THE DAILY FEAST

Everyday Meals We Love to Share

A Taste of Bulgaria, page 190.

THE DAILY FEAST

Everyday Meals We Love to Share

Esther Rose Graber

with

Ellen, Ann, Sibyl, Susan, Jane, and Yvonne

Photo Credits

Susan Graber Hunsberger: front dust jacket flap, opposite title page, pages 23, 24, 121-124, 127, 129, 130, 134, 136, 184, 187, 188, 191, 192, 194, 195, 198-200, 243

David Johnson: photos of authors on front and back covers, photo on pre-title page, pages 3-7, 25, 27, 34, 35, 41, 53, 56-58, 76, 77, 83, 96, 109, 116, 117, 133, 138, 139, 153, 156, 161, 167, 172, 177, 178, 208, 219, 223, 228, 251, 252

Kevin Montague: food photos on back cover, back dust jacket flap, pages 8-10, 14, 17-21, 26, 33, 36, 39, 40, 42, 45, 48, 50, 54, 55, 60, 62-64, 67, 69, 70, 73, 74, 78, 81, 82, 84, 87-90, 92-94, 98, 99, 101, 104, 107, 110, 113-115, 118, 119, 140, 142, 165, 168, 171, 174, 180, 196, 203, 204, 206, 211, 212, 220, 224, 226, 229, 230, 233, 235, 238-241, 246, 249

Debby Wolvo: pages 145, 146, 148, 149, 151, 152, 154, 157, 158

Supplied by Esther Rose and Ron Graber: pages 31, 72, 86, 143, 211

Supplied by Ann and Keith Graber Miller: page 106

Allison Douglass: food-stylist for photos on pages 8, 18-21, 26, 33, 36, 39, 40, 45, 50, 54, 55, 62-64, 67, 70, 73, 74, 81, 82, 84, 87, 89, 90, 94, 98, 99, 101, 104, 110, 113-115, 119, 140, 171, 174, 180, 203, 204, 206, 212, 220, 226, 229, 230, 233, 235, 239, 240

Book Design: Cliff Snyder

THE DAILY FEAST

Copyright © 2015 by Esther Rose Graber

Good Books books may be purchased in bulk at special discounts for sales promotion, corporate gifts, fund-raising, or educational purposes. Special editions can also be created to specifications. For details, contact the Special Sales Department, Good Books, 307 West 36th Street, 11th Floor, New York, NY 10018 or info@skyhorsepublishing.com.

Good Books in an imprint of Skyhorse Publishing, Inc.®, a Delaware corporation.

Visit our website at www.skyhorsepublishing.com.

10 9 8 7 6 5 4 3 2 1

Library of Congress Cataloging-in-Publication Data

The daily feast : everyday meals we love to share / by Esther Rose Graber ... [et al.].

p. cm.

Includes index.

ISBN 978-1-56148-756-1 (hardcover : alk. paper) 1. Cooking. I. Graber, Esther Rose.

TX714.D352 2012

641.5--dc23   2011053335

Paperback ISBN: 978-1-56148-821-6

Printed in China

Contents

Introduction

THE WOMEN IN OUR FAMILY utterly love to cook! There are seven of us – mother, five daughters, one daughter-in-law – and although none of us is professionally trained, we all have a love for cooking. We create, experiment, and share our best recipes with each other, always striving for that "perfect" meal. Over the years we have produced several photocopied collections that are constantly in use in all of our homes, functioning as our primary cookbooks. Because of the positive response we've had from friends and guests who have shared our tables and requested recipes (the meals that get the "wow!" response), we've arranged our best-loved recipes and menus into a book that we hope will be helpful, easy, and a pleasure for you to use.

Our food memories and experiences as a family go back more than 80 years, to the days of pap, cambric tea, and impossibly hot curries. Our heritage is rooted in Amish and Mennonite cooking that unites families and friends around the shared pleasures of the table, but our tastes have expanded through a love of travel. That began with Grandpa Joe and Grandma Minnie Graber, who spent many years in India and brought us their love for Indian cuisine, which Grandma prepared with great skill.

From left to right: Ellen, Sibyl, Susan, Esther Rose, Jane, Ann, and Yvonne.

Our immediate family lived and worked in Puerto Rico, where husband and dad, Ronald Graber, was a surgeon for 35 years, so our children developed a special fondness for the local dishes of the Caribbean. Since then, Ron and I, our children and their spouses, and our grandchildren have lived or spent significant time in many places, including Italy, Spain, England, Germany, Cambodia, China, the Dominican Republic, Bulgaria, Turkey, Greece, Indonesia, New Zealand, and Mexico. From many of these countries come some of our favorite recipes for fabulous dishes, which we've included in this book.

In this collection, each of us cooks shares three complete menus – one for a Soup Meal, the second for a Family Weeknight Supper, and the third for a more elaborate Guest Dinner.

If you have ever wondered what to serve with a particular dish to round out your menu, we have some ideas! Each meal takes into account the ease of preparation, balance of textures and flavors, and eye appeal. Partly because we're a family of artists – watercolorists, book illustrators, potters, designers, musicians – we know these meals will look as beautiful as they taste.

In addition to our cooks' special meals, we also offer our favorite Special-Occasion Meals. Our family reunions always feature an Indian or Puerto Rican meal, with each family preparing one or more of the dishes on the menu.

For us, it's not only about the *eating*, but also *preparing* the meal, a collective and delightful process when we're all together. Because many of these dinners have particular memories attached to them, we tell our stories here, too, all bits of our family legacy.

In our homes, the men cook, too. When I was a little girl, the only times I remember seeing Papa in the kitchen were when he was passing through, after washing up at the porch pump, heading for the dinner table. But one day, there was Papa in the kitchen, sitting on the kitchen chair with Mama on his lap! I can still remember the wonderful feeling, after all these years (that was back in the 1930s when I was a very small child), of the loving warmth of their arms welcoming me into the middle of their embrace.

Ann and Esther Rose

The roles of men and women were clearly defined in those days. Mama's place was in the kitchen, the home, and garden. Papa's was out in the world where he worked on cars and trucks and brought home a paycheck. And on Sundays he preached at the small Mennonite country church where he was pastor.

In Ron's and my home these roles were a given. I took care of the home and children, while my husband was a busy doctor and surgeon.

Then our daughter Ellen got married (she was the first of our six to marry), and we visited the newlyweds in their home in Vermont. Imagine my surprise at seeing Nelson in the kitchen, wearing an apron, working at the stove with total aplomb. As other men came into the family, we quickly discovered they were quite adept in the kitchen. Now we count on them to do the grilling, and on occasion, to produce a complete meal.

Following family tradition, the grandchildren are developing their own specialties in the kitchen, and they may someday produce a cookbook of their own. But that will be another story.

In the meantime, don your aprons and join us. We hope you have as much fun in the kitchen as we do! And we wish you great success in creating beautiful meals to be shared and enjoyed by your family and friends.

Esther Rose Graber

From left to right: Sibyl (partially hidden), Ann, Ellen, Esther Rose, and Jane, cooking together in Sibyl's kitchen.

CHAPTER 1

Esther Rose Graber

BORN DURING the Great Depression and raised on simple country cooking (I loved Mama's Sunday pot roast, fried chicken, and mincemeat pie), I discovered beautiful food at a friend's table in Scottdale, Pennsylvania, where I was working as an illustrator for the Mennonite Publishing House. Not only was it my first taste of shrimp and avocados (heavenly!), but the colorful and luscious arrangement on the salad platter opened my eyes to food as an art form. That dinner was an epiphany of sorts, setting me on a lifetime course of recipe-collecting and cooking.

My mother-in-law, Minnie Graber, whose pies were unparalleled, set standards for guest meals that were a challenge to a young bride-to-be. I didn't want my new husband, Ron, to be yearning for his mother's cooking. But she generously shared her recipes and techniques. Now, after all of these years, I'm still trying to impress Ron, and he's my best critic and fan combined.

Favorite Soup Supper

Potato, Kale, and Sausage Soup

Pear and Gorgonzola Salad
with Orange Dressing

Rustic Italian Bread

Mrs. Rohrer's
Lemon Sponge Pie

Potato, Kale, and Sausage Soup

Serves 6   •   Prep. Time: 20 minutes   •   Cooking Time: 50-60 minutes

½ lb. bulk sausage (spicy, hot, sage, medium, Italian, — whichever you prefer)

1½ cups chopped onion

1 Tbsp. vegetable oil

4-5 small, new red potatoes, scrubbed, quartered, unpeeled

4-6 cups chicken broth, depending on the consistency you like

1-3 cups kale, ribs removed, leaves thinly sliced, according to the amount of vegetables you like

1 cup milk

2 Tbsp. cornstarch, dissolved in ¼ cup water

½ tsp. salt, or to taste

freshly ground black pepper

1. Fry the sausage until brown and crumbly. Set aside.

2. In a medium soup kettle, sauté the onion in the vegetable oil until soft.

3. Add the potatoes and the broth and bring to a boil.

4. Add the kale and the browned sausage. Cook until the potatoes are tender.

5. Stir in the milk.

6. Bring just to a boil. Stir in the cornstarch mixed with water. If you want a soup with more body, use an additional tablespoon of cornstarch.

7. Add salt and a generous grind of pepper. Taste and adjust the salt.

COOK'S NOTE
I like to cook a whole pound and freeze half for a quicker soup later.

COOK'S NOTE
Optionally, use one large, red potato, scrubbed, quartered, and thinly sliced or cubed. Do not peel. In a pinch you can substitute other potato types, peeled and thinly sliced, but your soup will lack the lovely bits of color.

EVERYONE *in our family loves this hearty soup. The sausage and kale are a great flavor combination, and the red skin of the potato adds an extra note of color.*

THIS IS A *great salad combination, plus the dressing is suitable for any salad that includes fruit. We think it goes especially well with D'Anjou pears.*

Pear and Gorgonzola Salad with Orange Dressing

Serves 6 • *Prep Time: 30 minutes*

THE ORANGE DRESSING

¼ cup raspberry, or
red wine, vinegar

⅓ cup olive oil

¼ cup frozen orange
juice concentrate,
undiluted

½ tsp. grated orange rind

1 Tbsp. fresh lemon, *or*
lime, juice

1-2 tsp. sugar, to taste

½ tsp. hot pepper sauce,
or more, to taste

¼ tsp. salt, or to taste

1. Combine all dressing ingredients in a small jar with a lid. Shake well.

2. Transfer to a small pitcher. Give the dressing a stir before pouring.

> ∨ COOK'S NOTE
> *Use your favorite combination of available greens. Fresh lettuce leaves and baby spinach make a beautiful background for the pears.*

THE SALAD

6 cups salad greens

3 ripe D'Anjou pears

½ cup, or more,
Gorgonzola cheese
crumbles

1 cup toasted pecans or
Honey Cayenne Pecans
(see page 238)

chives or green onions,
optional

1. Divide the greens evenly among 6 salad plates, or place on one large platter.

2. Peel and remove cores from pears. Slice into quarters.

3. Arrange pears atop the greens.

4. Sprinkle the Gorgonzola over the pears.

5. Scatter the pecans over the salads.

6. Sprinkle with snipped chives or green onions, if desired.

7. If serving individual salads, pass the dressing to let persons serve themselves. If arranging one platter, drizzle dressing over the salad just before serving.

Rustic Italian Bread

Makes 1 loaf • *Prep Time: 10 minutes* • *Rising Time: 2 hours* • *Baking Time: 25-35 minutes*

3½ cups bread flour

2 tsp. sugar

1 scant tsp. salt

1 package (1 Tbsp.) active dry yeast

2 Tbsp. olive oil

1 cup, plus 2 Tbsp., warm water

You'll also need 2-4 Tbsp. cornmeal, part of an egg white, and some coarse salt for the finishing

1. Place all ingredients (except cornmeal, egg white, and coarse salt) in your bread machine. Process on dough setting.

2. Meanwhile, sprinkle an ungreased baking sheet with cornmeal.

3. When the dough is ready, turn it out onto a lightly floured surface. If it's sticky, knead in a little additional flour. Let it rest for 15 minutes, then shape into a long loaf.

4. Transfer to the baking sheet, cover with a towel, and let rise in a warm place until doubled, 30-40 minutes.

5. Heat oven to 375°.

6. With a sharp knife, make several diagonal slashes across the loaf. Brush with beaten egg white. Sprinkle lightly with coarse salt.

7. Bake for 25-35 minutes, or until loaf is lightly browned and gives a hollow sound when tapped lightly.

A BREAD MACHINE *makes this so easy. Just put everything into the machine, turn it to "dough" setting, and let the machine do the work. This recipe produces a chewy, crusty loaf that is great alongside hearty, rustic Potato, Kale, and Sausage Soup.*

Mrs. Rohrer's Lemon Sponge Pie

Serves 6 • Prep Time: 30 minutes • Baking Time: 35-40 minutes • Standing Time: 15 minutes

1 cup sugar

3 Tbsp. flour

1 large egg, separated

1 tsp. grated lemon rind

2 Tbsp. lemon juice (a little extra won't hurt!)

2 Tbsp. melted butter

1 cup milk

pinch of salt

1 unbaked 9-inch pie crust (see page 15)

COOK'S NOTE

I like to partially bake the pie shell before filling in order to avoid a doughy bottom. To pre-bake the crust, prick all over with a fork and bake at 400° for 10 minutes. Remove from the oven, and reduce the oven temperature to 350°. Immediately fill the crust with the prepared filling and return to the oven for 35-40 minutes, or until puffy and slightly browned on top.

1. Combine the sugar and flour in a medium-sized bowl.

2. Beat in the egg yolk, lemon (or lime) rind, and juice.

3. Add the melted butter. Stir in the milk.

4. In a separate bowl, beat the egg white with a pinch of salt until fairly stiff. Fold into the lemon mixture until no streaks of white show.

5. Pour into an unbaked 9" pie crust.

6. Bake at 350° for 35-40 minutes, or until crust is lightly browned and filling is puffy and touched with brown. Let cool for about 15 minutes before cutting.

COOK'S NOTE

When we had a productive lime tree near our house in Puerto Rico, I would substitute limes for the lemon in this recipe with great success.

WE'VE NEVER MET *Mrs. Rohrer, a Mennonite woman who was featured, along with her recipes, in a Family Circle magazine article many years ago. This is one of her recipes that has become a family favorite, not only for its simplicity and economy (only one egg!), but because it is always delicious.*

Whether you make it with lemons or limes, serve it still warm from the oven or chilled, the fresh, light, custard-bottom pie is simply delectable. Dress it up with a dollop of whipped cream and a scattering of raspberries or blueberries if you're serving guests. This one is always a winner!

As a young bride, *I wanted to learn to make a pie that lived up to the quality of my mother-in-law's pies. The challenge was formidable. Her pies were perfection, and they were my husband's favorite dessert!*

I had almost decided it couldn't be done, since every pie crust recipe I tried turned out either too tough or too crumbly. It wasn't that my mother-in-law didn't share her recipes: I just didn't have her touch. Until! - I discovered hot water pastry. But even then, that recipe tells you to chill the dough before rolling it out, and that didn't work for me.

I finally perfected an easy, non-fail pie-crust recipe, and I've been using it successfully for - well, years and years. The neat thing about this dough is that you can keep re-working it without damaging the flakiness. So if it tears a bit, just rearrange the pieces, patch it together and keep going. You're going to have a delicious pie!

Mom's Pie Crust

Makes two 8" or 9" pie crusts, or one 10" deep-dish pie crust with some pie dough left over

⅔ cup vegetable
shortening, plus
2 Tbsp.

1 scant tsp. salt

⅓ cup boiling water

2 cups all-purpose
flour, *divided*

1. Place the vegetable shortening into a small metal bowl.

2. Add the salt.

3. Pour the boiling water over the shortening and salt. Using a fork and a spatula, combine the shortening, salt, and hot water. Use the fork to whip it into a creamy emulsion.

4. Add 1½ cups of the flour to the emulsion, combining well.

5. Gradually add up to ½ cup more of the flour, a little at a time, being sure to keep the mixture soft and pliable. (If you add too much flour at this point it will get dry and crumbly and you'll have to start over. It's happened to me!)

6. Roll out the dough between two sheets of waxed paper dusted with flour. If the dough sticks to the paper add a bit more flour.

   (If you're making a 10" deep-dish crust, you'll have enough dough to roll it beyond the edges of the waxed paper. Just save those extra pieces and form them into a ball. More later about what to do with them!)

7. Peel off the top sheet of waxed paper, replace it lightly, then flip the whole thing over and peel off the other side. Now flip it again onto your hands and ease into the pie pan. Remove the final sheet of paper once you've eased the crust into the pan. If it tears a bit or doesn't quite fit, don't worry, just patch it up.

8. Roll out the ball of extra dough (see Step 6). Cut it into strips about 1" wide. Sprinkle with sugar and cinnamon. Bake in a small pan along with the pie until brown. Or make the strips into a braid to decorate the edge of the pie.

COOK'S NOTE
My preferred vegetable shortening is Crisco, either plain or butter-flavor. Use real butter for part of the shortening in this recipe if you want a more decadent pie.

Favorite Family Supper

Lemon-Barbecued Meat Loaves

Creamy Corn Bake

Wilted Spinach Salad with
Hot Bacon Dressing

Oven Fries
(recipe not included; use your own favorite)

Grandma Minnie's
Open-Face Apple Pie

WHEN I ASKED *my husband Ron to choose his favorite family meal from a broad selection, this meat loaf dinner was Ron's first choice. Full of comfort food that is reminiscent of his past, it includes a corn pudding and wilted spinach and bacon salad. Naturally it has to be topped off with Grandma Minnie's open-face apple pie!*

This is not a 30-minute meal, so why not invite friends over, since you're going to want to share all this goodness. Add oven fries, roasted new potatoes (page 199), or simple baked potatoes if it's a company meal.

Lemon-Barbecued Meat Loaves

Serves 6 • *Prep. Time: 30 minutes* • *Baking Time: 35-40 minutes*

4 slices day-old bread, cut or torn into cubes

¼ cup lemon juice

¼ cup minced onion

1 egg, slightly beaten

2 tsp. salt

1 tsp. lemon pepper, *optional*

1 tsp. grated lemon rind, *optional*

1½ lbs. ground beef

1 lemon, sliced into 6 rounds

THE SAUCE

½ cup ketchup

⅓ cup brown sugar

1 tsp. dry mustard

¼ tsp. allspice

¼ tsp. ground cloves

1. In a large bowl combine the bread cubes, lemon juice, onion, egg, and salt.

2. Add the lemon pepper and lemon rind, if you wish. Mix well and set aside. Wait to mix in the ground beef until you've prepared the sauce.

3. Prepare the sauce. Combine the ketchup, brown sugar, dry mustard, allspice, and cloves.

4. Add **half** of this mixture to the bread/egg mixture. Reserve the other half of the sauce for the meat loaf topping.

5. Combine the ground beef with the bread/egg/sauce mixture.

6. Shape into 6 small individual loaves.

7. Place in a 9" × 13" baking pan.

8. Cover the loaves with the reserved sauce. Top each with a slice of lemon.

9. Bake at 350° for 35-40 minutes.

CHAPTER 1
ESTHER ROSE'S
MENU

FAVORITE
FAMILY
SUPPER

Creamy Corn Bake

Serves 8 • *Prep. Time: 20 minutes* • *Baking Time: 45-50 minutes*

¼ cup flour

¼ cup cornmeal

½ tsp. baking powder

1 tsp. sugar or more, to taste

½ tsp. salt or more, to taste

2 large eggs

15½-oz. can whole-kernel corn, drained

14½-oz. can cream-style corn

1 cup milk

3 Tbsp. butter, melted

freshly ground black pepper, to taste

COOK'S NOTE

If you can't get the canned, cream-style corn, just open a can of whole-kernel corn and buzz it with a hand-blender directly in the can until creamed.

1. Generously grease either a 2-quart casserole or 8 ramekins.

2. In a small bowl, combine the flour, cornmeal, baking powder, sugar, and salt.

3. In a large mixing bowl, beat the eggs. Then stir in the well-drained whole-kernel corn, the cream-style corn, and the flour/cornmeal mixture.

4. Stir in the milk and the melted butter.

5. Check the seasonings, adding salt and sugar to taste. Add a few grinds of fresh black pepper.

6. Pour the mixture into a single casserole, or divide between 8 ramekins. Bake at 350° until set in the center and nicely puffed and browned, 45-50 minutes, or until a knife inserted in the center comes out clean.

THIS LOVELY CASSEROLE *is almost a soufflé. If you want to get fancy and take this to another level, you could add sautéed onion, and sautéed green and red peppers to the corn mixture, and top it off with a handful of shredded Jack cheese.*

Wilted Spinach Salad with Hot Bacon Dressing

Serves 6-8 • Prep. Time: 15 minutes • Cooking Time: 30 minutes

3-4 slices smoked bacon, cut into 1" pieces

1 small onion, chopped

1 Tbsp. flour

2 Tbsp. sugar + 1 tsp.

½ tsp. salt

3 Tbsp. cider vinegar

1 cup water

10-oz. bag fresh spinach (about 6-8 cups of leaves)

1-2 eggs, hard-boiled, *optional*

1. Fry the bacon pieces in a medium skillet until nicely browned, 10-15 minutes. Remove from the skillet and drain on paper towels.

2. In the drippings remaining in the skillet, sauté the onion until translucent.

3. Stir in the flour, combining well.

4. In a small bowl or 2-cup measuring cup, combine the sugar, salt, vinegar, and water.

5. Pour into the skillet and stir constantly until the sauce thickens and comes to a boil. Boil gently for two minutes.

6. To serve, pour the hot dressing over the fresh spinach leaves and toss to combine.

7. Transfer to a serving dish and top with the reserved bacon bits. Decorate with the sliced eggs, if desired. Serve immediately while warm.

THIS IS ONE *of our favorite ways to serve spinach. Grandma Minnie used to make this often by sight and feel, nothing written down, and no measuring equipment in evidence. Of course it was always delicious. Here's my version of the dressing, with measurements.*

Grandma Minnie *always cut her pies into quarters for serving if there were three or four of us at the table. No matter how much you protested, you were going to have a quarter of a pie set in front of you. (Of course, secretly, we really did want a quarter of whatever pie Grandma had baked.) Now when we make this pie, we serve ourselves standard pieces, but we keep cutting ourselves little extra slices, until we've basically each had a quarter of the pie! When it's still warm from the oven, it's especially hard to resist.*

Grandma Minnie's Open-Face Apple Pie

CHAPTER 1

ESTHER ROSE'S
MENU

FAVORITE
FAMILY
SUPPER

Serves 4-8 • *Prep. Time: 35 minutes* • *Baking Time: 50-60 minutes*

1 unbaked 9" pie crust
(see Mom's Pie Crust,
page 15)

¾ cup sugar

⅓ cup flour

2 Tbsp. butter

4-6 apples, peeled, cored,
and sliced, or enough to
generously fill a 9"crust

cinnamon, *optional*

¼ cup water

2 Tbsp. lemon juice

⚠ VARIATION

*If the apples are very tart,
omit the water/lemon juice
and use ½ cup cream. Sprinkle
generously with cinnamon,
and bake as above.*

1. Blend the sugar and flour and sprinkle ¼ of this mixture on the bottom of the unbaked pie shell.

2. Cut the butter into the remaining flour/sugar mixture using a pastry cutter to make fine crumbs. Set aside.

3. Arrange the slices of apple over the sugar/flour in the pie crust.

4. Cover the apples with the reserved mixture of flour/sugar/butter. Sprinkle with cinnamon, if desired.

5. Combine the ¼ cup water with the lemon juice. Pour over the pie.

6. Bake at 425° for 15 minutes. Then reduce heat to 375° and continue to bake for 35-45 minutes. To test if the apples are done, poke a sharp knife into one of the slices near the center of the pie. It should pierce easily. Return to the oven for another 5-10 minutes if the knife meets resistance.

Favorite Guest Dinner

Marinated Roasted Olives

Herbed and Spiced Almonds

Green Beans with Citrus Butter

Turkish-Style Chicken, Lamb,
or Beef Kabobs

Turkish Ottoman Rice Casserole

Roasted Beet & Goat Cheese Salad
with Balsamic Dressing

Lemon Trifle

Marinated Roasted Olives

Makes 2 cups • *Prep. Time: 15 minutes* • *Baking Time: 15 minutes*

2 cups green and black olives of various sizes

2 Tbsp. olive oil

2 garlic cloves, minced

¼ tsp. dried oregano

¼ tsp. crushed red pepper flakes

¼ tsp. salt flakes, or ground salt

½ tsp. freshly ground black pepper

1 tsp. orange, or lemon, zest

1 Tbsp. finely chopped parsley

½ tsp. finely chopped rosemary

1. On a baking sheet, toss together the olives, oil, garlic, oregano, red pepper, salt, and black pepper.

2. Roast at 450° for about 15 minutes until sizzling hot and aromatic.

3. Transfer the hot olives to a serving bowl and toss in the zest, parsley, and rosemary. Serve warm or at room temperature.

WITH THIS starter there's no need for formalities ... guests can sip on a drink and nibble while standing around the kitchen island or the grill, watching the cook or the grill-master put finishing touches on dinner.

CHAPTER 1

ESTHER ROSE'S
MENU

FAVORITE
GUEST
DINNER

Herbed and Spiced Almonds

Makes 1 cup • *Prep. Time: 5 minutes* • *Cooking/Baking Time: 20-22 minutes*

2 tsp. olive oil

1 Tbsp. finely chopped
rosemary

1 tsp. rubbed (powdered)
thyme

¼ tsp. cinnamon

¼ tsp. cayenne pepper

¼ tsp. black pepper

¼ tsp. salt

1 cup raw unsalted almonds

1. In a medium saucepan over medium heat combine oil and all ingredients except almonds. Cook the herbs and spices, stirring frequently, for about 3 minutes.

2. Add the nuts and toss well to combine. Sprinkle with additional salt and cook another minute, stirring.

3. Spread nuts on a large rimmed baking sheet. Bake at 350º, stirring once after 7 minutes, until deeply browned and fragrant, about 10-12 minutes.

4. Cool on paper towels. Sprinkle with additional salt if desired. Pour into a pretty dish or basket lined with parchment paper.

COOK'S NOTE

These can be baked up to 3 days ahead and stored at room temperature in an air-tight container.

Green Beans with Citrus Butter

Serves 6-8 • *Prep. Time: 20 minutes* • *Cooking Time: 10 minutes*

1 pound fresh green beans, ends trimmed

1 Tbsp. olive oil

1 Tbsp. grated orange peel

2 tsp. grated lemon peel

2 garlic cloves, minced, *optional*

¼ cup chicken broth

2 Tbsp. butter

salt and pepper

1. Cook the beans in a large pot of boiling, salted water until barely tender (about 4 minutes). Drain well. If doing ahead, chill the beans quickly in a bowl of ice-water to stop the cooking.

2. Heat oil in a heavy, large skillet over medium-high heat. Add orange peel, lemon peel, and garlic, and stir one minute.

3. Add broth and simmer an additional minute.

4. Add butter and beans. Toss until beans are heated through and sauce coats the beans.

5. Season with salt and pepper and serve.

Grandchildren cool off in the pond at Sibyl's place.

MINT AND SPICES *in yogurt add a Turkish flair to this marinade. The flavors are perfect with chicken, lamb, or beef kabobs. You could also serve the marinade as a dip with pita bread and crudités.*

There is enough marinade in this recipe for 1½ lbs. of chicken, lamb or beef, with some remaining to serve on the side.

Turkish-Style Chicken, Lamb, or Beef Kabobs

CHAPTER 1

ESTHER ROSE'S
MENU

FAVORITE
GUEST
DINNER

Serves 6 • *Prep. Time: 25 minutes* • *Marinating Time: 1-4 hours* • *Grilling Time: 10-20 minutes*

1 cup plain yogurt

2 Tbsp. fresh lemon juice

1 tsp. grated lemon peel

1 cup chopped fresh mint

2 large garlic cloves, minced

1 tsp. salt

½ tsp. cinnamon

¼ tsp. cayenne pepper

¼ tsp. allspice

1½ lbs. lean chicken breast, lamb, or beef, cut into 1" cubes

1. Whisk yogurt, lemon juice, and peel in a small bowl until smooth.

2. Add mint, garlic, salt, cinnamon, cayenne, and allspice. Cover and chill for up to 24 hours.

3. Divide the marinade in half, reserving half for serving alongside the grilled meat.

4. In the remaining half of the marinade, marinate the chicken pieces, lamb, or beef for 1-4 hours, covered, in the refrigerator.

5. Remove from the marinade, leaving a thin coating of marinade on the meat. Pierce with skewers and grill, basting with marinade occasionally.

6. Serve the kabobs with the reserved half of the marinade alongside in a separate bowl.

COOK'S NOTE
If choosing beef, select only the most tender cuts, such as sirloin tips or filet mignon.

COOK'S NOTE
Any marinade that has come in contact with the raw meat should be boiled for 1 minute before you use it for basting the kabobs on the grill.

Esther Rose tending the stove.

CHAPTER 1

ESTHER ROSE'S
MENU

FAVORITE
GUEST
DINNER

Turkish Ottoman Rice Casserole

Serves 8 • Prep. Time: 15 minutes • Cooking Time: 50-60 minutes

THE BASIC RICE PILAF

2 Tbsp. butter

2 Tbsp. olive oil

1 small onion, diced

1-2 cloves garlic, minced

¼ tsp. turmeric

½-1 tsp. curry powder

2 cups uncooked long-grain rice

3½ cups chicken broth, or
3½ cups water plus 2 cubes
chicken bouillon

salt and pepper, to taste

COOK'S NOTE
*Be sure the broth has a good
rich taste as the rice will
absorb much of the flavor.*

1. In a deep skillet or large saucepan, heat the butter and olive oil until the butter melts.

2. Add the diced onion and sauté until the onion is transparent.

3. Add the minced garlic, the turmeric, and the curry powder, stirring for about 1 minute.

4. Stir in the rice and continue to sauté, stirring constantly until rice grains become opaque.

5. Pour in the chicken broth. Bring to a boil, uncovered, stirring to dissolve bouillon cubes if using.

6. Taste the broth. Add salt and pepper to taste.

7. Reduce heat to low, cover, and cook without stirring until rice is tender. Fluff the rice with a fork. If it is too dry and not quite tender, add a bit of water and cover again over low heat.

8. Now add the extras suggested below that will turn this into a special company dish.

THE EXTRAS

½-1 cup toasted, slivered almonds, or pistachios

½-1 cup dried cherries, cranberries, or currants

½ cup toasted pine nuts

COOK'S NOTE
*Currants are
the genuinely
Turkish
addition.*

Transfer the finished pilaf to a handsome, well-buttered casserole. Top with the béchamel sauce, opposite.

Turkish Ottoman Rice
Caserole, continued

When Ron and I *visited Istanbul, Turkey, with our daughter Susan and her family, they introduced us to one of their favorite restaurants, Asitane.*

The Asitane staff was attempting to reproduce the lost cuisine of the great Ottoman Empire. The Cook's Guild of the empire guarded their secret recipes with their lives, so written recipes did not exist. The Asitane staff had extensively researched the kitchen records of the royal palace, Topkapi, and the ledgers of the Cook's Guild.

The dishes they developed for their menu were unusual, with many exotic combinations. Everything we tasted was delicious. One dish, called Kadirga Pilaf, was a standout, and we've reproduced it for our guest menu with great success. It is based on a simple rice pilaf recipe, but the additions elevate its status to a dish fit for the Grand Pasha himself.

THE BÉCHAMEL SAUCE

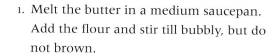

2 Tbsp. butter

2 Tbsp. flour

1½ cups milk

½ tsp. salt

1 Tbsp. grated Parmesan cheese, *optional*

1. Melt the butter in a medium saucepan. Add the flour and stir till bubbly, but do not brown.

2. Add the milk all at once and stir constantly until smooth and thick. Stir in the salt and the Parmesan cheese. Taste for seasoning

3. Pour the béchamel over the finished Pilaf.

4. Just before serving, slip under the broiler until the top is bubbly and beautifully browned.

COOK'S NOTE

To make the Casserole ahead of time, make the pilaf, add the extras, and pour the béchamel sauce over top. It can sit up to 2 hours at room temperature. Thirty minutes before serving, put the casserole dish into a 350° oven for 20 minutes to heat it up. Then run it under the broiler as explained in step 4 above. Serve.

CHAPTER 1
ESTHER ROSE'S
MENU

FAVORITE
GUEST
DINNER

Roasted Beet & Goat Cheese Salad with Balsamic Dressing

Serves 8 • Prep. Time: 20 minutes • Baking Time: 30-50 minutes • Chilling Time: 1 hour

THE BEETS

8 small to medium-sized beets
(1½-2" in diameter)

⚠ COOK'S NOTE

You can substitute canned beets if you're short of time. Marinate them in some of the dressing at least 30 minutes before arranging your salad.

1. Trim off the beet greens, leaving on the tails and an inch of stem. Rinse the beets.

2. Place the beets in a baking pan with ¼" water. Cover tightly.

3. Bake the beets for 30-50 minutes at 375° until they are tender when pressed gently or pierced with a knife.

4. Cool to room temperature.

5. Peel, and slice into rounds, about ¼" thick. Cover and chill.

WHEN FRESH BEETS *are available, home-roasted beets are a special treat, and you can roast them a day or two before your dinner party. Feta cheese or fresh mozzarella cubes could be substituted for the goat cheese when that isn't available or doesn't suit your budget. Here's where you should use the best balsamic vinegar you have and a top quality olive oil – blood-orange is our favorite, when we can get it.*

THE BALSAMIC DRESSING

2 Tbsp. balsamic vinegar

¼ tsp. salt

¼ cup olive oil

2-3 Tbsp. blood-orange olive oil, if available; or several drops of concentrated orange, or lemon, oil, if available; or top quality olive oil of your choice

¼ tsp. lemon, or orange, zest

Shake all the ingredients together in a small jar with a tight-fitting lid. Chill.

Roasted Beet & Goat Cheese Salad
with **Balsamic Dressing**, continued

THE COMPOSED SALAD

a bed of mixed greens, red and green lettuce, spinach, arugula - your choice

the roasted, sliced beets

1 medium red onion, thinly sliced, separated into rings

2 oz. goat cheese, crumbled, or small cubes of fresh mozzarella cheese

1 cup walnuts, toasted

1. On eight individual salad plates, or a large platter, create a bed of greens.

2. Arrange the slices of beets, alternating with red onion rings.

3. Drizzle the balsamic vinaigrette over the beets and onion rings.

4. Crumble goat cheese over all. Scatter generously with the toasted walnuts.

Never a wasted moment.
Grandma Minnie.

CHAPTER 1

ESTHER ROSE'S
MENU

FAVORITE
GUEST
DINNER

Lemon Trifle

Serves 8-10 • *Prep. Time: 45 minutes* • *Cooking Time: 25 minutes* • *Chilling Time: 12 hours*

THE CANDIED LEMON PEEL AND SYRUP

4 lemons

3 cups sugar, *divided*

2 cups water

1. Using a vegetable peeler, remove peel from lemons in long strips, end to end, yellow parts only. Reserve lemons for Curd (see below).

2. Blanch peel by placing in a small saucepan. Add enough cold water to cover generously. Bring to a boil.

3. Drain off the water. Repeat blanching two more times.

4. Now cut the lemon peel into ⅛" wide strips.

5. In a separate pan, combine 2 cups sugar with 2 cups of water, stirring until the sugar dissolves to create the syrup. Boil gently for 5 minutes.

6. Add the lemon peel and simmer until the peel is translucent, about 15 minutes.

7. Using a slotted spoon, transfer peel to a small baking sheet lined with foil. Sprinkle up to 1 cup of the reserved sugar over the peel and toss to coat.

8. Let dry at room temperature 2 hours.

9. Transfer lemon peel to an airtight container. Pour cooled syrup into a glass jar. Refrigerate.

THE LEMON CURD

4 large egg yolks

2 large eggs

¾ cup sugar

½ cup fresh lemon juice
(from the above
4 lemons)

pinch of salt

1. Prepare double boiler or place a metal bowl on top of a pan of simmering water. The bowl should fit tightly and not touch the water.

2. Whisk together the ingredients in a separate bowl.

3. Place mixture into top of double boiler over simmering water.

4. Whisk constantly, until mixture thickens and registers 160° on a candy thermometer, approximately 6-8 minutes.

5. Transfer to a glass bowl. Place plastic wrap directly on the surface, and refrigerate overnight or longer.

Lemon Trifle, continued

THE TRIFLE

candied lemon peel,
divided

lemon curd, *divided*

2 cups chilled
whipping cream

42 soft ladyfingers
(from two 3-oz.
packages)

lemon syrup, *divided*

1. Place large metal bowl and beaters for whipping cream in freezer for at least 20 minutes.

2. Finely chop enough candied lemon peel to measure ¼ cup. Place in a small bowl.

3. Mix ½ cup lemon curd into the chopped lemon peel. Cover and chill.

4. Beat whipping cream in chilled bowl until stiff.

5. Fold 1 cup of whipped cream into remaining lemon curd. Cover and chill.

6. Cover and chill remaining whipped cream.

7. Line a trifle dish or glass bowl with ladyfingers around the sides and bottom.

8. Brush generously with the lemon syrup.

9. Place half the lemon-cream mixture over the bottom layer of ladyfingers.

10. Top with a layer of whipped cream, and then another layer of ladyfingers. Brush with syrup.

11. Repeat, topping final layer with the lemon curd/peel mixture.

12. Pile any remaining whipped cream around the outside edge of trifle. Cover and refrigerate.

13. Just before serving, sprinkle remaining candied lemon peel on top.

AFTER A VISIT, *a friend called this "...one of the best desserts we have ever had!"*

Make the candied lemon peel, syrup, and lemon curd two or three days in advance. Put it all together the day before or the morning of your dinner. Totally worth the time and effort.

CHAPTER 2

Jane Graber Davis

JANE, OUR FIRST-BORN, lives with her husband, Scott Davis, a lighting director, in Nashville, Indiana. She is a potter. As a specialist in miniature Early American ware, Jane is well-known in her field and has been featured in several North American ceramics magazines.

Each fall, when the native Brown County trees are in full color, Jane hosts an open house. Her studio displays miniature rooms featuring her redware, salt-glazed, and stoneware pottery, as well as other renowned miniaturists' work. At the event, Jane's close friends set out a gourmet buffet for visitors and collectors from across the U.S. The day after the show, we serve a brunch to those friends. Our favorite brunch recipes are in Chapter 14, beginning on page 222.

When Jane prepares a lunch for the volunteers at the Brown County Habitat for Humanity, she usually concocts a hearty soup. Our favorite is her version of Spicy Lentil Soup. When she and Scott entertain at home, Scott prepares the grilled food. Note the beautiful grilled salmon for Jane's guest dinner.

Favorite Soup Supper

Spicy Lentil Soup

Parmesan Herb Bread

Evie's Fresh Spinach Salad

Mom's Apple Crisp
with **Cranberries**

———————— ❧ ————————

THIS HEARTY SOUP *has become a standby in Jane's kitchen. It's one of the favorite lunches for the crew of Habitat for Humanity in Brown County, Indiana.*

When there are vegetarians among the builders, Jane simply substitutes vegetable broth for the chicken broth.

This is a thick soup, so you can add extra broth or water to extend it if you wish. Be sure to check for salt if you add water. If you have meat-lovers in the family, you could add slices of kielbasa or smoked sausage before serving.

Spicy Lentil Soup

Serves 8 • Prep. Time: 20 minutes • Cooking Time: 2 ½ hours

4 cups chopped onion, about 2 large onions

¼ cup olive oil

4 tsp. minced garlic, about 4 cloves

1½ cups finely chopped celery, about 3 ribs

1½ cups finely chopped carrots, about 3 carrots

1 tsp. curry powder

1 tsp. cumin

1 tsp. salt

1 tsp. black pepper

½ tsp. dried thyme

5 cups chicken, beef, or vegetable broth

2 bay leaves

2 tsp. brown sugar

2 Tbsp. ketchup

3 cups canned tomatoes, chopped

2 cups lentils, rinsed

5 cups water

½ cup dry sherry

1. Sauté onions in olive oil in large kettle until softened.

2. Add garlic, celery, and carrots. Cook 10-15 minutes, stirring frequently.

3. Add all seasonings and sauté briefly.

4. Add the broth, bay leaves, sugar, ketchup, tomatoes, lentils, water, and sherry.

5. Simmer 2 hours, or until lentils are very soft, stirring occasionally. Add extra water if needed.

6. Taste for salt and adjust seasoning. Remove bay leaves before serving.

Parmesan Herb Bread

Serves 8-15 • *Prep Time: 15-20 minutes* • *Baking Time: 20 minutes*

2 1-lb. loaves
brown-&-serve
French bread

THE BUTTER MIXTURE

1 stick (½ cup) butter,
softened

¼ cup grated Parmesan
cheese

4 Tbsp. snipped
fresh parsley

1 tsp. dried oregano

¼ tsp. garlic salt

1. In a small bowl, combine the butter, Parmesan cheese, parsley, oregano, and garlic salt, mixing well.

2. Cut loaves into ½"-¾"-thick slices, not cutting through bottom crust.

3. Butter one side of each slice thickly with the mixture, spreading a little over tops of loaves.

4. Wrap loaves in foil.

5. Bake at 400° for 10 minutes. Unwrap. Bake 10 minutes longer.

6. To serve, complete the cuts between slices in the kitchen. Place slices in a basket. Or if the supper is very casual, serve the loaves on cutting boards with a bread knife for diners to serve themselves.

EVERYONE LOVES *this flavorful bread, served hot and crusty straight from the oven. We think it's the perfect accompaniment to an Italian dinner and often make the simplified version to go with a soup supper.*

THE SIMPLIFIED VERSION

1 or 2 loaves fully baked
Italian or French bread

1. Split the loaves lengthwise.

2. Follow directions above for the butter mixture.

3. Spread the mixture thickly over the cut surface of each piece of the bread.

4. Place bread pieces cut-side up on baking sheet.

5. Broil, watching carefully, until crisply browned.

6. Cut into serving pieces and serve immediately.

Evie's Fresh Spinach Salad

Serves 6 • *Prep Time: 20-30 minutes*

THE SALAD

2 oranges

6-8 cups spinach greens, washed and dried

½ cup chopped dates

1 small red onion, sliced in rings

THE DRESSING

2 Tbsp. lemon juice

½ tsp. salt

1 tsp. Worcestershire sauce

¼ tsp. freshly ground pepper

¼ cup salad oil

½ tsp. sesame oil

¼ tsp. orange zest (from above)

1-2 Tbsp. toasted sesame seeds

1. Zest one orange to obtain ¼ teaspoon zest. Set aside. Peel both oranges. Section with a sharp knife, removing membranes if desired. Set aside. Save any accumulated juice to add to the dressing.

2. In a salad bowl, layer spinach, oranges, dates, and onion rings.

3. Whisk together in a small bowl the lemon juice, salt, Worcestershire, pepper, salad oil, sesame oil, the reserved orange zest, and any accumulated orange juice.

4. Just before serving, toss the dressing with the salad ingredients.

5. Top with the toasted sesame seeds. Serve.

SUSAN WROTE, *"This was my favorite when you used to make it, Mom, and it's become my own family favorite since. Guests can't get enough. It really is an addictive combination."* The recipe originally came from a dear friend, Evie Kreider.

39

Mom's Apple Crisp with Cranberries

Serves 8-10 • *Prep. Time: 15 minutes* • *Baking Time: 35-45 minutes*

4 cups sliced, or diced, apples

¾ cup sugar

1 Tbsp. flour

⅛ tsp. salt

½ tsp. cinnamon

½ cup cranberries, fresh or frozen

¾ cup dry oatmeal, rolled or quick

¾ cup flour

¾ cup brown sugar

⅛ tsp. baking powder

⅓ cup (5⅓ Tbsp.) butter

½ cup chopped walnuts

generous dash of cinnamon

1. Combine the apples, sugar, 1 Tbsp. flour, salt, ½ tsp. cinnamon, and cranberries. Mix well.

2. Place in a greased 9"×13" casserole or baking pan.

3. In a separate bowl combine the oatmeal, ¾ cup flour, brown sugar, and baking powder.

4. Cut in the butter with a pastry cutter or two knives until crumbly.

5. Spread over the apple mixture in the pan or casserole.

6. Sprinkle on the walnuts and cinnamon.

7. Bake, uncovered, at 375° for 35-45 minutes, or until apples are tender when pricked with a fork.

THIS DESSERT *is easier to make than a pie and probably better for you, too. Serve warm with a dip of ice cream.*

Favorite Family Supper

Linguini with
Fresh Tomato Sauce

Basil & Walnut Pesto

Grilled Romaine Salad

Maple Yogurt with Berries

———

IN THE SUMMER, *the tomatoes in Jane's garden practically explode off the vines in a great wealth of color and flavor. Nearby, the basil plants are full and bountiful. Now is the time to enjoy fresh tomato sauce and fresh pesto!*

Linguine with
Fresh Tomato Sauce

Serves 6 • *Prep. Time: 30 minutes* • *Cooking Time: 30 minutes*

½ cup finely chopped onion

4-6 cloves garlic, minced

2 Tbsp. olive oil

8 cups peeled, seeded, chopped, and drained ripe tomatoes (about 6 lbs.), *divided*

1 tsp. salt

½ tsp. black pepper

½ cup sliced, pitted, ripe olives

½ cup snipped fresh basil

12 oz. linguini, or spaghetti

freshly shaved, or grated, Parmesan cheese

△ COOK'S NOTE

We prefer the Di Giorno brand of fresh pasta when we can get it.

1. In a large saucepan, cook onion and garlic in hot oil until tender but not brown.

2. Stir in half the tomatoes. Add the salt and pepper.

3. Bring to a boil. Reduce heat.

4. Simmer, uncovered, for 15 minutes, stirring occasionally.

5. Stir in the remaining 4 cups tomatoes, the sliced ripe olives, and the fresh basil. Heat through.

6. Meanwhile, cook the linguini or spaghetti according to package directions. Drain.

7. Serve the tomato sauce over the pasta. Sprinkle with freshly shaved or grated Parmesan cheese.

HOW TO PEEL AND SEED TOMATOES FOR SAUCE:

1. With a sharp knife, make a shallow X on the bottom of each tomato.

2. Using a slotted spoon or steamer basket, dip the tomatoes into a pan of boiling water for about 10-15 seconds.

3. Rinse with cold water. Allow to cool slightly.

4. Now pull off the skin, starting at the X. The skin should come off easily.

5. Cut the tomato in half crosswise. Scoop out the seeds and discard.

6. Chop seeded tomato. Place in a sieve or colander over a bowl to drain off excess juice. You may save the juice to add later to the sauce if you want it to be juicier.

Basil and Walnut Pesto

Makes 2 cups • *Prep. Time: 10 minutes*

2 cups fresh basil leaves,
washed and patted dry

4 large cloves garlic

1 cup walnuts

1 cup best-quality olive oil

1 cup freshly grated
Parmesan cheese

¼ cup freshly grated
Romano cheese

pinch of salt

fresh ground pepper, to taste

1. Bring a pot of water to boil. Prepare an ice-water bath. Now plunge the basil leaves into the boiling water for 3-5 seconds, then immediately into the ice-water bath (this preserves their bright green color). Pat dry.

2. Combine the basil, garlic, and walnuts in the bowl of a food processor. Chop briefly.

3. Leave the motor running and add the olive oil in a slow, steady stream. Turn off the processor.

4. Add cheeses, a big pinch of salt, and a liberal grinding of pepper.

5. Process briefly to combine.

6. Scrape into a bowl and cover until ready to use. This is enough to sauce 2 pounds of pasta.

We sometimes briefly sauté in butter sliced zucchini, peppers, and onions from the garden. To the sauté we add some sliced fresh mushrooms, plus this pesto, and top pasta with the mix. A wonderful garden supper! You can freeze any extra pesto.

Pasta with Pesto

Serves 6-8 • *Prep. Time: 5 minutes* • *Cooking Time: 8-13 minutes, depending on the pasta*

¼ cup heavy cream

2 Tbsp. hot pasta cooking water

1 cup pesto

1 lb. pasta, cooked and drained

freshly grated Parmesan cheese

1. Combine the cream, pasta water, and 1 cup pesto in a large serving bowl.

2. Add pasta and toss until well-combined. Pass Parmesan at the table.

Grilled Romaine Salad

Serves 8 • Prep. Time: 15 minutes • Grilling Time: 20 minutes

6 Tbsp. extra-virgin olive oil

2 Tbsp. red wine vinegar

1 Tbsp. chopped fresh mint

1 tsp. lemon zest

2 Tbsp. fresh lemon juice

2 tsp. Dijon mustard

1 garlic clove, finely chopped

salt and pepper

2 hearts romaine lettuce,
quartered lengthwise, with
some stem attached to
hold the lettuce together

1 large red onion cut into
½" thick rounds

8-oz. package grilling cheese, or
queso blanco, cut into ¼" slices

1. Whisk oil, vinegar, mint, mustard, lemon zest and juice, mustard, and garlic in small bowl. Season to taste with salt and pepper.

2. Brush lettuce and onion slices with dressing. Sprinkle with salt and pepper.

3. Oil the grill before heating. Grill onion slices until charred in spots and softened, about 5 minutes per side. Keep the grill lid open.

4. Transfer onion slices to cutting board, and cut into bite-sized chunks. Transfer to salad bowl.

5. Grill lettuce until charred in spots and slightly wilted, about 2 minutes per side with the grill lid open.

6. Transfer to a cutting board and cut into bite-sized pieces. Discard the root. Add the lettuce pieces to the bowl.

7. Grill the cheese slices until charred in spots and softened, about 2 minutes per side with the grill lid open.

8. Cut into bite-sized pieces and add to salad bowl.

9. Dress with additional dressing. Pass any additional dressing at the table.

I COULDN'T IMAGINE *how you could grill lettuce with good results, but it's absolutely delicious. There's something about that smoky, grilled flavor with the touch of mint and lemon in the dressing that makes this recipe stand out. Do persuade your grill-master to be brave and try this.*

Maple Yogurt with Berries

Serves 4-6 • *Prep. Time: 5 minutes*

COOK'S NOTE

*Jane prefers
thick, creamy
Greek yogurt.
Or use low-fat
yogurt by
draining it
in a paper-
towel-lined
strainer for
at least half
an hour.*

1 cup plain yogurt

2 Tbsp. maple syrup

Assorted fresh berries
in season

Stir the maple syrup into the plain
yogurt. Spoon over your selection
of fresh berries.

WHAT *could be simpler than this?
And positively delicious!*

*Jane's miniature stoneware, wheel-thrown and hand-painted,
in one-inch scale (standard dollhouse scale).*

Favorite Guest Dinner

Hummus

Bourbon-Glazed Salmon with
Sesame Seeds

Brown and Wild Rice Pilaf with
Toasted Pecans

Mixed Snap Peas and Baby Peas

Strawberry and Goat Cheese Salad
with Raspberry Dressing

Grandma's Rhubarb Cream Pie

Hummus

Serves 8-10 • *Prep Time: 5-10 minutes*

¼ cup tahini (sesame paste)

¼ cup fresh lemon juice

1-2 cloves garlic, peeled and crushed

½ tsp. salt

¼ tsp. cumin

15-oz. can garbanzo beans, drained

olive oil for garnish

paprika for garnish

chopped fresh parsley, for an appetizer

diced red, yellow, and green bell peppers, for a salad

grilled chicken, for a salad

mixed greens, for a salad

1. For an appetizer, put tahini, lemon juice, garlic, salt, and cumin in food processor. Blend until smooth.

2. Add the beans. Blend to a smooth paste.

3. To make an appetizer platter, spoon hummus onto a serving plate. Sprinkle paprika on top. Surround with a ring of chopped parsley. Drizzle some of your best olive oil over all. Serve chilled, with wedges of pita and fresh vegetables.

4. For a salad, add water, a bit at a time, until the hummus reaches the consistency of heavy cream. Combine with diced red, yellow, and green bell peppers and grilled chicken on a bed of mixed greens for an excellent luncheon salad.

COOK'S NOTE
Add a roasted red pepper or two with the garbanzos in Step 2. It makes a delicious variation with a lovely color.

WHETHER IMPRESSING *a crowd with one large salmon fillet, or preparing individual portions as outlined below, the procedure is the same. It's also worth noting that the bourbon glaze marinade in this recipe is quite delicious on chicken and pork.*

COOK'S NOTE

There are various methods for preparing this salmon – and they're all good: you'll just have to decide which one suits you best. Susan likes the effects of direct heat on Jane's bourbon glaze, and she puts her salmon under the broiler so the whole surface of the fish becomes caramelized with sizzled edges. To get the same caramelization plus a nice smoky flavor on the grill, she uses a grilling basket so the fish can be flipped. She serves the fillets with the crispy skin on, as her family enjoys the taste and nutritional benefits from an occasional serving of fish skin.

Bourbon-Glazed Salmon with Sesame Seeds

Serves 8 • *Prep Time: 10 minutes* • *Marinating Time: 30 minutes* • *Grilling Time: 9-11 minutes*

½ cup packed
brown sugar

6 Tbsp. bourbon

¼ cup soy sauce

2 Tbsp. fresh lime juice

2 tsp. grated, peeled,
fresh ginger

½ tsp. salt

½ tsp. ground
black pepper

2 garlic cloves, crushed

8 5-oz. salmon fillets,
about 1" thick

cooking spray or oil

4 tsp. sesame seeds

½ cup thinly sliced
green onions

1. Combine sugar, bourbon, soy sauce, lime juice, ginger, salt, pepper, and garlic in a large zip-top plastic bag.

2. Add salmon fillets. Marinate in refrigerator 30 minutes, turning bag once.

3. Remove fillets from bag. Set aside on plate.

4. Pour marinade into a saucepan and boil three minutes.

5. Place fillets skin-side down onto well-oiled grill on medium-high heat.

6. Close grill cover to help steam the salmon. Check for doneness in the center after 7-8 minutes. The thin ends of the fish will get done faster than the thick center. Total time may take 9-11 minutes. Do not overcook.

7. Remove finished salmon from grill to a warm serving platter. Lift it carefully off the skin with a spatula, leaving the skin on the grill to be cleaned later.

8. Before serving, spoon some of the boiled marinade over the salmon.

9. Garnish with the sesame seeds and green onions.

ALTERNATE BROILER METHOD

1. Preheat broiler.

2. Place fillets, skin-side down, on broiler pan coated with cooking spray.

3. Broil 11 minutes, or until fish flakes easily when tested with a fork.

4. Follow steps 8 and 9, above.

Brown and Wild Rice Pilaf with Toasted Pecans

Serves 6-8 • *Prep. Time: 10 minutes* • *Cooking Time: 55-65 minutes*

8 cups water

⅔ cup uncooked wild rice

1⅓ cups uncooked brown rice

½ cup coarsely chopped pecans

1 Tbsp. butter

½ tsp. salt

½ tsp. freshly ground black pepper

parsley sprigs

1. In a large saucepan, bring water to a boil.

2. Add the wild rice and cook uncovered over moderate heat for 15 minutes.

3. Add the brown rice and continue cooking, uncovered, for 20 minutes more.

4. Drain off and reserve the cooking water. Transfer the rice to a steamer or colander.

5. Return the hot water to the large saucepan.

6. Set the rice in its colander over the boiling water. Cover. Steam in this manner for 15-20 minutes, or until the rice is tender.

7. Meanwhile, toast the pecans on a baking sheet in a 300° oven, stirring occasionally, for 10-15 minutes. Set aside.

8. To serve, transfer the rice to a warm serving bowl, gently stirring in the butter, salt, pepper, and toasted pecans. Garnish with parsley sprigs.

COOK'S NOTE

Consider turning any leftovers into a delicious rice salad by adding sliced green onions and a light dressing.

THIS DISH *is the perfect foil for the Bourbon-Glazed Salmon. Don't skip the steaming step. The result is a tender rice with just the right crunchiness added by the toasted pecans. Lovely!*

Mixed Snap and Baby Peas

Serves 6-8 • *Prep: 10 minutes* • *Cooking Time: 5-8 minutes*

3 cups frozen baby peas

2 cups fresh snap peas, strings removed

butter to taste

salt to taste

1. Cook frozen baby peas according to package directions.

2. Add fresh snap peas just before serving, tossing only long enough to heat through.

3. Season with butter and salt to taste.

The Graber women with some of their artistic work, together in Sibyl's studio.

Strawberry & Goat Cheese Salad with Raspberry Dressing

Serves 6-8   •   *Prep. Time: 10 minutes*

1 Tbsp. Dijon mustard

1 Tbsp. raspberry balsamic vinegar

1 Tbsp. white balsamic vinegar

¼ cup olive oil

¼ cup canola, or vegetable, oil

¼ cup Chambord, *optional*

¼ tsp. salt

6-8 cups salad greens

1 pint strawberries, sliced

crumbled goat cheese, to taste

1. Combine the Dijon mustard, the two vinegars, olive oil and salad oil, plus the Chambord (if using), and the salt in a small jar and shake well. Chill.

2. Arrange the greens on 6-8 individual salad plates.

3. Top with sliced strawberries and crumbled goat cheese.

4. Pass the chilled dressing.

Grandma's
Rhubarb Cream Pie

Serves 6-8 • *Prep Time: 15 minutes* • *Baking Time: 50-60 minutes*

3 cups rhubarb, cut into ½" pieces

1½ cups sugar

3 Tbsp. flour

¼ tsp. nutmeg

2 eggs, well beaten

1 Tbsp. butter, melted

9" unbaked pastry shell
(see page 15)

1. Place rhubarb in pastry shell.

2. In a small bowl, combine the sugar, flour, nutmeg, beaten eggs, and melted butter.

3. Pour the mixture over the rhubarb. If desired, top with pastry cut-outs or lattice.

4. Bake at 400° for 10 minutes. Then reduce oven temperature to 350° and bake for an additional 40-45 minutes.

5. Check the center of the pie to make sure the filling is completely set. This can be deceptive, as the top forms a crust. With a knife, poke under that crust in the center of the pie to check for doneness. If it's still looking runny there, pop it back in the oven for another 5-10 minutes.

6. Serve warm or cold.

THIS IS *one of our favorites of Grandma Minnie's pies, and it is all the reason you'll need to run out and plant a patch of rhubarb in your garden.*

CHAPTER 3

Ellen Graber Kraybill

Ellen followed her father into the medical field as a physical therapist. She is also the musician in the family, singing soprano in a professional choral group and leading music at her congregation in Elkhart, Indiana.

For five years, Ellen served on staff at the London Mennonite Centre in England, helping host visitors from around the world. She and her husband, Nelson Kraybill, a pastor, author, and former seminary president, entertain frequently, so her recipe book is bulging with menus.

When daughters Laura and Andrea are home, you will often find them with Ellen in the kitchen being creative. Nelson brings in extra chairs or presides at the grill. Their dining table is a place of family bonding, deepening friendship, storytelling, and lots of laughter.

Favorite Soup Supper

Lemon-Mint Iced Tea

Warm Naan Bread

Senegalese Soup

Wedge of Iceberg with
Ranch or Italian Dressing

Fresh Strawberry or Peach Pie

Lemon-Mint Iced Tea

1 gallon • *Prep Time: 5 minutes* • *Steeping Time: 30 minutes*

4 quarts water, *divided*

one big handful of fresh mint leaves on stems, washed

5 decaffeinated black tea bags

12-oz. can frozen lemonade concentrate

additional fresh mint leaves, *optional*

1. Bring 2 quarts of water to a boil.

2. Place the fresh mint and the tea bags in a stainless steel pot.

3. Pour the boiling water over the tea bags and mint and allow to steep for 30 minutes.

4. Strain.

5. Add the frozen lemonade to the tea mixture.

6. Stir in the additional 2 quarts water to make 1 gallon tea.

7. To serve, pour over ice and garnish with fresh mint leaves, if desired.

The garden at Sibyl's home.

Naan Bread

Serves 6 • *Prep. Time: 20 minutes* • *Rising Time: 2½ hours* • *Baking Time: 4 minutes*

3 cups sifted flour

1 tsp. baking powder

1¼ tsp. dry yeast

1 egg

½ cup, plus about 3 Tbsp.,
warm milk, *divided*

¾ tsp. salt

2 tsp. sugar

2 Tbsp. vegetable oil

4 Tbsp. plain yogurt

poppy seeds, or white onion seeds

THIS IS *a traditional
recipe for Naan bread.*

1. In a large bowl, whisk together the flour, baking powder, and yeast. Set aside.

2. Beat the egg in another bowl. Add the ½ cup warm milk, salt, sugar, oil, and yogurt to egg.

3. Add the egg mixture to the flour mixture, adding the additional warm milk as needed. Knead for 10 minutes.

4. Coat the ball of dough lightly with oil. Let rise, covered with a damp towel, for two hours.

5. Shape into six balls. Let rise again for 15 minutes covered with a towel.

6. Shape each ball of dough into a tear-drop shape about 4"×10".

7. Put three of these on a baking sheet, brush each with water, leaving a ¼ inch margin around the outside edge.

8. Top with poppy seeds or white onion seeds. Let rise again 15 minutes.

9. Broil on high for 2 minutes, or until lightly brown.

10. Flip and broil on other side.

THIS AFRICAN-INSPIRED soup receives an added dimension of richness by toasting the peanut butter before adding it to the soup. Sprinkled generously with the garnishes, the warm, spicy, and cool combination delights the palate.

Senegalese Soup

Serves 6 • Prep: 15 minutes • Cooking Time: 1 hour

1 large onion, diced

5 Tbsp. olive oil, *divided*

2 tsp. chopped garlic

2-3 Tbsp. curry powder,
depending on your
spiciness preference

2 tsp. ground coriander

6 cups chicken broth

1 cup, or 8-oz. can, tomato sauce

2 cups crushed or diced tomatoes

1 tsp. sugar

½ cup smooth peanut butter

1 lb. boneless chicken breast,
cooked and diced,
about 2 cups

salt and pepper to taste

1 cup scallions, thinly sliced

chopped peanuts

chopped cilantro

1. Cook onions in 3 Tbsp. oil until translucent. Add garlic. Cook 2 minutes.

2. Add curry powder and ground coriander and fry for 2 minutes, stirring constantly.

3. Add broth, tomato sauce, crushed tomatoes, and sugar. Simmer slowly, covered, for 30 minutes, stirring frequently. Do not let soup boil vigorously.

4. In a small skillet, heat remaining 2 Tbsp. oil. Add peanut butter and cook over low heat, stirring constantly for about 5 minutes. Be careful not to let it burn!

5. Place about 2½ cups of the soup in a blender. Add the hot peanut butter-mixture.

6. Start on very low speed, holding lid in cocked position. Blend the peanut butter with the soup until mostly smooth. A bit of texture is desirable. Return to soup kettle.

7. Stir in the diced chicken and heat through. Taste for salt and add along with pepper as needed.

8. Serve in bowls garnished with a generous sprinkling of scallions, chopped peanuts, and chopped cilantro.

COOK'S NOTE
Leftover rotisserie chicken, a mixture of dark and light meat, is perfect for this.

61

I**F STRAWBERRIES** *are at their peak in your local gardens, it's time to have fresh strawberry pie. You'll love the consistency of this pie and its gorgeous red color. Served with a dollop of whipped cream and a fresh, whole strawberry on top, this is truly a spring treat. (But we confess to sometimes having it in mid-winter made with hothouse berries.)*

Fresh Strawberry Pie

Serves 6-8 • *Prep. Time: 20 minutes* • *Cooking Time: 10 minutes* • *Chilling Time: 2-4 hours*

¾ cup sugar

¼ cup white corn syrup

3 Tbsp. cornstarch

1 cup water

4 Tbsp. strawberry-flavored
gelatin powder

1 Tbsp. fresh lemon juice

3 cups sliced, fresh strawberries

1 baked 8" or 9" pie shell
(see page 15)

8 whole strawberries

△ COOK'S NOTE

*For a fresh peach-pie variation,
follow the recipe exactly, except
substitute best-quality peaches
and peach-flavored gelatin.*

1. Combine the sugar, white corn syrup, cornstarch, and water in a small saucepan, blending well.

2. Cook over high heat, stirring constantly, until mixture comes to a boil. Reduce heat. Continue to cook and stir until mixture is thick and clear, another minute or two. Remove from heat.

3. Stir in the strawberry gelatin powder until completely dissolved.

4. Add the lemon juice. Cool for at least 10 minutes.

5. Gently fold the sliced berries into the sauce. Spoon evenly into the pie shell.

6. Cover with plastic wrap. Chill for several hours.

7. Serve each slice topped with whipped cream and garnished with a whole, fresh strawberry.

Favorite Family Supper

Nelson's Calico Baked Beans

Tropical Cornbread

Cabbage Patch Coleslaw

Honey Lime Fruit with
Fresh Mint (see page 119)

Nelson's Calico Baked Beans

Serves 8 • *Prep. Time: 10 minutes* • *Cooking/Baking Time: 1½ hours*

¼ lb. smoked bacon, diced

½ lb. ground beef

1 medium onion, chopped

2 16-oz. cans pork and beans, undrained

15-oz. can kidney beans, or red beans, undrained

15-oz. can lima beans, or Northern white beans, undrained

½ cup brown sugar

½ cup ketchup

½ tsp. salt

2 Tbsp. yellow mustard

1 Tbsp. Worcestershire sauce, *optional*

2 Tbsp. smoky BBQ sauce, *optional*

1. In a large skillet, fry together bacon, ground beef and onion until well browned. You may fry the bacon first for a few minutes, and drain off some of the fat if you wish before adding beef and onion.

2. Add all beans with their juices. Stir in the remaining ingredients.

3. Transfer to a greased, large, shallow casserole, (a 9" × 13" baking dish works well), pulling some of the bacon pieces to the top.

4. Bake for 1½ hours at 325°.

COOK'S NOTE

This works well in a slow cooker, too. Drain liquid from bean cans before adding to the slow cooker. Cook on low for 3-5 hours.

WHEN WE FIRST *visited newlyweds Ellen and Nelson in Vermont, I was impressed with their kitchen collaboration, but apprehensive about the dish Nelson was preparing. I had a long-standing prejudice against pork and beans. However, the delicious bean casserole he served changed forever my childhood aversion to baked beans.*

This is one of the best baked bean casseroles ever. Ellen and Nelson have made this without meat and declare it is still delicious. It is a great dish for a potluck dinner.

Tropical Cornbread

Serves 8-10 • *Prep. Time: 15 minutes* • *Baking Time: 1 hour*

COOK'S NOTE

*If you want
to cut back on
the butter, use
only one stick
of butter and ¼
cup of vegetable
or canola oil.
The cornbread
will be a bit
more crumbly,
but just as
delicious.*

COOK'S NOTE

*If you don't have
canned cream-
style corn, buzz
a can of regular
corn, along
with its liquid,
to a creamy
consistency,
using your stick
blender or a
food processor.*

1 cup all-purpose flour

1 cup cornmeal

2 Tbsp. baking powder

1 tsp. salt

1½ sticks (¾ cup) butter,
room temperature

⅓ cup sugar

3 eggs

1½ cups cream-style corn

½ cup canned crushed
pineapple, well drained

1 cup shredded Monterey Jack,
or mild cheddar, cheese

1. Butter and flour a 9" square cake pan.
   (Glass is best, but you can use a metal pan.)

2. Whisk together the flour, cornmeal, baking
   powder, and salt in a medium bowl. Set
   aside.

3. Cream the butter and sugar till fluffy. Add
   the eggs, one at a time, beating well after
   each addition.

4. Add the corn, pineapple and cheese,
   mixing to blend.

5. Carefully add the dry ingredients and mix
   until blended.

6. Pour the batter into the prepared pan.
   Bake at 325° about 1 hour, until golden
   brown around the edges and a toothpick
   stuck in the center comes out clean.

THIS NEW TWIST *on cornbread, with its
addition of crushed pineapple and grated
cheese, makes it a standout and the perfect
accompaniment to Calico Baked Beans.*

Cabbage Patch Coleslaw

Serves 6 • Prep. Time: 15 minutes

3 cups shredded green cabbage

½ cup snipped fresh parsley

½ cup sliced green onions

2-3 Tbsp. sugar

3 Tbsp. cider vinegar

2 Tbsp. canola, or vegetable, oil

1 tsp. salt

1. In a medium bowl, combine the cabbage, parsley, and green onions.

2. In a separate small bowl combine the sugar, vinegar, oil, and salt for the dressing.

3. Toss the dressing with the cabbage mixture. Refrigerate until ready to serve.

THE COMBINATION *of shredded cabbage with snipped parsley, green onions, and light dressing, make this a delectably fresh and zingy alternative to the usual creamy coleslaws. This is a perfect go-along with the Calico Beans and the Tropical Cornbread. The recipe comes from Grandma Minnie's collection.*

Favorite Guest Dinner

Roasted Red Pepper,
Almond, & Cilantro Pesto

Pita Crisps (see page 89)

Grilled Lime-Dijon Pork Tenderloin

Yukon Gold Mashed Potatoes

Steamed Asparagus

Mixed Greens with Grapes
and Citrus Vinaigrette

Amaretto Baskets with Berries

Roasted Red Pepper, Almond, and Cilantro Pesto

2 cups • *Prep. Time: 10 minutes*

16-oz. jar roasted red peppers, drained, or
roast your own (see page 133)

1 cup cilantro leaves

1 Tbsp. tomato paste

1 Tbsp. sherry vinegar, or red wine vinegar

2 Tbsp. fresh lemon juice

2 cloves garlic, minced

scant ½ tsp. salt

¼ tsp. sugar

1 tsp. paprika, hot or sweet

1 tsp. chili powder

¼ tsp. cayenne

1 cup coarsely chopped, toasted almonds

COOK'S NOTE
*Toast the almonds at 350° in the oven
for 8-10 minutes, or in an ungreased
skillet, stirring or tossing until
light brown and aromatic.*

1. Put all ingredients in a food processor bowl.

2. Process until smooth. Taste for salt and cayenne, and adjust to taste.

3. This can be refrigerated for up to 3 days. To preserve the lovely color, cover the surface of the pesto with plastic wrap.

4. Bring to room temperature to serve. Serve with pita crisps (see page 89), crostini, or crackers.

Grilled Lime-Dijon Pork Tenderloin

Serves 6 • *Prep. Time: 15 minutes* • *Marinating Time: 30 minutes-2 hours* • *Grilling Time: 12-15 minutes*

2 pork tenderloins (¾ lb. each)

2 Tbsp. honey

⅓ cup fresh lime juice

½ tsp. cumin

¼ cup olive oil

1 tsp. black pepper, coarsely
ground

½ tsp. salt

dash of cayenne - about ⅛ tsp.

1 Tbsp. Dijon mustard

1 tsp. fresh garlic, minced

1 tsp. grated lime peel

1. Pierce tenderloins in several places with a sharp knife.

2. Combine the honey, lime juice, cumin, olive oil, pepper, salt, cayenne, Dijon, garlic, and grated lime peel to make the marinade.

3. Place the tenderloins in a large plastic food bag with the marinade and seal tightly.

4. Marinate for at least 30 minutes and up to two hours.

5. Remove the tenderloins from the marinade, reserving the marinade in a small saucepan.

6. Place the tenderloins on a pre-heated grill. Cook on medium high for about 3 minutes per side, turning 4 times, and basting with the reserved marinade. The pork is done when a cooking thermometer inserted in the thickest part reaches 150°.

7. Let rest 10 minutes, covered with foil, before cutting.

8. Heat the marinade to boiling and boil for two minutes. Drizzle the boiled marinade over the sliced pork to serve.

WE RETURN *to this marinade recipe over and over, occasionally changing the finishing sauce to, for example, the Bourbon glaze on page 51.*

Yukon Gold
Mashed Potatoes

Serves 8-10 • *Prep. Time: 25 minutes* • *Cooking Time: 15-25 minutes*

5 lbs. Yukon Gold potatoes

half stick (¼ cup) butter, softened

4 oz. cream cheese, softened

½-1 cup sour cream, *divided*

½-1 tsp. salt, depending on your
taste preference

THESE MASHED POTATOES
*will make you happy. The
Yukon Golds are a lovely,
pale gold color and whip up
beautifully. Of course, there
are other potatoes that will
work well for mashing,
but these are special
if you can get them.*

1. Peel the potatoes, cut into 2" chunks, and place in stockpot. Add water to barely cover potatoes.

2. Bring to a boil. Continue to cook with the pot partially covered until potatoes become very tender, about 15-25 minutes. Stop cooking and remove from the water before potatoes get mushy. Reserve cooking water.

3. Whip with the paddle beater of your electric mixer, or mash with a potato masher by hand.

4. Add the butter, cream cheese, ½ cup sour cream, and salt.

5. Whip until smooth and fluffy, adding more sour cream or potato cooking water to lighten if the potatoes seem too stiff. Taste for salt and add more if needed.

6. Transfer to a heated serving bowl. Cover and keep warm until ready to serve.

The Graber family after Sunday service at "Iglesia Menonita de Aibonito," 1966.
From left to right: Ellen, Sibyl, Susan, Ann, Ron, Jane, Steven, Esther Rose.

Mixed Greens with Grapes and Citrus Vinaigrette

Serves 8 • *Prep. Time: 20 minutes*

¼ cup light olive oil, or canola oil

1½ Tbsp. cider vinegar

1 Tbsp. fresh lime, or lemon, juice

1½ Tbsp. sugar

⅛-¼ tsp. salt, to taste

4-6 cups mixed salad greens

1½ cups grapes, halved

½ cup sliced green onions

½-1 cup toasted pecans
(or Honey Cayenne Pecans, page 238)

1. Combine the oil, vinegar, lime or lemon juice, sugar, and salt in a small bowl. Whisk.

2. Arrange the greens on a large plate. Scatter the grapes, green onions, and toasted pecans over the greens.

3. Drizzle the dressing over all.

△ COOK'S NOTE

To toast the pecans, spread them out on a baking sheet and toast in a 350° oven for about 10 minutes. Or wrap in paper towels and microwave on high for 1-2 minutes, depending on strength of your microwave.

COOK'S NOTE

You can usually find packages of salad greens in the grocery store called Mesclun Mix. Or make your own mix of red and green lettuce, arugula, mizuna, frisee, cress, escarole, baby beet greens, etc.

THIS LOVELY *no-bake dessert combines a creamy,
frozen base with a bounty of fresh summer berries.
The frozen baskets can be stored, well-wrapped, in
the freezer for several weeks.*

OUR FAVORITE BERRY COMBINATION

2 cups hulled, diced, fresh strawberries, or 2 cups fresh peaches, diced
1 cup fresh blueberries
1 cup fresh raspberries
¼-½ cup sugar

1. Combine the berries and add ¼ cup sugar or more, to taste. Mix gently.
2. Let stand to release juices, mixing occasionally, about 30 minutes.

Amaretto Baskets
with Berries

Serves 8–10 • *Prep. Time: 20 minutes* • *Freezing Time: 2 hours* • *Standing Time: 30 minutes*

8-oz. package cream cheese, not fat-free, at room temperature

½ cup sugar

¼ cup Amaretto

1 cup chilled whipping cream

△ COOK'S NOTE

You can substitute frozen whipped topping, thawed, for the whipped cream in this recipe, but do not use the fat-free variety, or your baskets will turn into puddles! If you do substitute whipped topping for the whipped cream, reduce the amount of sugar in the baskets to ¼ cup.

1. Choose a cookie sheet or tray that will fit in your freezer. Line it with foil.

2. Place a large metal mixing bowl in freezer to chill.

3. Using an electric mixer, beat the cream cheese in a medium bowl until smooth.

4. Beat in ½ cup sugar, and then the Amaretto.

5. Using the same beaters, beat whipping cream in the large, chilled bowl until peaks form.

6. Fold whipped cream into cheese mixture in two additions.

7. Drop cheese mixture in small mounds on the foil-lined pan. Make a total of 8-10 mounds.

8. Using the back of a spoon, make a depression in the center of each mound, pressing to form 2½"-3"-diameter baskets.

8. Freeze baskets until firm, at least 2 hours. Then wrap well and store in freezer until ready to use.

9. To serve, place each basket on a dessert plate. Allow to thaw slightly. Fill generously with the fresh fruit (opposite), about ½ cup per serving.

COOK'S NOTE △

In winter months, frozen berries can stand in for the fresh.

CHAPTER 4

Sibyl Graber Gerig

SIBYL, AN ARTIST and illustrator, lives with her family in a passive solar home surrounded by acres of reclaimed Indiana prairie. The family's chickens, goats, and garden provide fresh farm-to-table ingredients for much of the creative cooking happening in the kitchen.

Trained as a medical illustrator, Sibyl has illustrated numerous texts, including three children's books. She currently creates watercolors as well as fabric art, working from her home studio.

Sibyl is the mother of Hannah, Adrienne, Emma, and Madeline. Sibyl spent many enjoyable hours in the past 25 years, preparing meals for and with her growing children and her surgeon husband, as well as hosting many of the larger family gatherings.

Always on the lookout for the perfect recipe, she enjoys trying out recipes from around the world. Our best Chinese dinners are served from Sibyl and Winston's kitchen, with Winston manning the woks and all the women at the chopping boards. One of Sibyl's family's favorite soups is a spicy Mexican Posole, and if you're invited to dinner, expect something possibly exotic and definitely delicious.

Favorite Soup Supper

Mexican Posole Stew

Cheese Quesadillas
(see page 142)

Lemon Panna Cotta with
Sweet Balsamic Glaze

or

Brownie Pudding

THIS WONDERFUL, *hearty soup makes a full meal – no salad necessary. For guests, Sibyl serves simple cheese quesadillas on the side (page 142), but plain warm flour tortillas are just as good.*

Mexican Posole Stew

Serves 8-10 • *Prep. Time: 30 minutes* • *Cooking Time: 2 hours*

2-3-lb. pork loin roast, fat trimmed off

9½ cups water, *divided*

2 tsp. salt

2 Tbsp. olive oil

1½ cups coarsely chopped onion

4 large garlic cloves, minced

1½ serrano chiles, seeds and ribs removed, minced

2 poblano peppers, seeds and ribs removed, chopped

8 tomatillos, husked and chopped

2 14-oz. cans white hominy, rinsed and drained, *divided*

juice of 1 lime

1-2 cups chopped cilantro

ACCOMPANIMENTS

1 cup sliced radishes

2 cups grated, or crumbled, queso blanco

lime wedges

tortilla chips

chopped cilantro

avocado chunks

1. In a large pot or Dutch oven, cover pork loin with 8 cups water and salt.

2. Bring to a boil, then cover partially and simmer over low heat until tender, 1½ hours. Alternatively, use a slow cooker on low for 5-8 hours.

3. Remove the meat from the broth, cool slightly, and pull apart, shredding the meat. Set aside the shredded meat.

4. Skim the fat from the broth. Discard fat. Set broth aside.

5. In a medium saucepan, heat the olive oil and sauté the chopped onion, garlic, serrano chiles, and peppers until soft. Add tomatillos and sauté until soft.

6. Add 2 cups of reserved broth and 1 can drained hominy to the sautéed mixture. Purée with a stick blender, leaving some chunks. Alternatively, transfer mixture to a blender and purée.

7. Return the puréed vegetables to the large pot, along with the shredded meat, the remaining 1½ cups water, and remaining hominy.

8. Add the lime juice and cilantro. Taste, adjusting salt. Serve with accompaniments.

COOK'S NOTE
You can also use pork butt or pork shoulder roast in this recipe. Do not use pork tenderloin or smoked pork.

Lemon Panna Cotta with Sweet Balsamic Glaze

Serves 8 • *Prep. Time: 5 minutes* • *Standing Time: 25 minutes*
Cooking Time: 15 minutes • *Chilling Time: 2-4 hours*

1 cup whole milk, *divided*

2½ tsp. (1 envelope) unflavored gelatin

2½ cups heavy whipping cream

½ cup sugar

strips of peel from one lemon, removed with a vegetable peeler

1 vanilla bean, split lengthwise

COOK'S NOTE

If you cannot get a vanilla bean, substitute ½ teaspoon vanilla extract.

1. Pour ½ cup milk into a medium bowl. Sprinkle gelatin over top. Let sit until gelatin softens, about 15 minutes.

2. Meanwhile, combine the remaining ½ cup milk with the cream, sugar, and lemon peel in a large saucepan. Scrape the seeds from the vanilla bean into the saucepan with the milk mixture. Add the vanilla bean itself.

3. Bring to a simmer over medium heat, whisking until sugar dissolves. Remove from the heat before it comes to a boil. Cover and let steep for 10 minutes.

4. Bring cream mixture back to a simmer. Add gelatin mixture and stir until dissolved. Strain through a sieve into a bowl with a pouring spout.

5. Pour equally among eight ramekins or custard cups.

6. Chill, uncovered, until panna cotta is set, 2-4 hours. Then cover and keep chilled. You can make these up to two days ahead of time.

7. To serve, use a sharp knife to cut around the edges of each panna cotta. Place a small serving plate atop each ramekin and invert, allowing panna cotta to settle onto the plate. Serve with a generous drizzle of the Sweet Balsamic Glaze, with additional glaze in a small pitcher to pass at the table.

Sweet Balsamic Glaze

Prep. Time: 5 minutes • Cooking Time: 30-40 minutes

1 cup dry red wine

⅓ cup balsamic vinegar

½ cup sugar

1. Bring wine, vinegar, and sugar to a boil in a 3-quart heavy, nonreactive saucepan over moderate heat, stirring until sugar dissolves.

2. Lower heat and continue to simmer, uncovered, stirring occasionally, for about 30 minutes, until reduced by about half, or until it is a syrupy consistency.

3. Allow to cool before serving.

SIBYL *doesn't often spend time making desserts, so when a fantastic dessert is a snap to prepare and gets a "wow" response, it's easy to see why she loves this recipe. Perfect for a guest dinner finale, it's a great do-ahead dessert, too.*

Brownie Pudding

Serves 8 • *Prep. Time: 15 minutes* • *Baking Time: 40-45 minutes*

1 cup all-purpose flour

2 tsp. baking powder

½ tsp. salt

¾ cup granulated sugar

2 Tbsp. cocoa powder

½ tsp. cinnamon

½ cup milk

1 tsp. vanilla

2 Tbsp. melted butter,
or margarine

¾ cup chopped nuts, *optional*

TOPPING

¾ cup brown sugar

¼ cup cocoa powder

1¾ cups strong, hot, decaf coffee

1. In a mixing bowl, whisk together the flour, baking powder, salt, granulated sugar, cocoa powder, and cinnamon.

2. Add milk, vanilla, and melted butter. Mix until smooth. Add nuts if you wish.

3. Pour batter into a greased 8" square baking pan.

4. In a separate small bowl, mix the brown sugar and cocoa powder together.

5. Sprinkle evenly over the batter.

6. Pour the hot coffee over the entire batter. Do NOT stir! At this point it looks like a mess, but don't worry, magic happens!

7. Bake at 350° for 40-45 minutes, or until the top is dry. Serve warm.

THIS IS A GREAT DESSERT *to make with kids, not only because it's simple, but it's also amazing to see how the baking process transforms separate ingredients into cake and sauce – like magic.*

We've given this recipe, from our friend Evie Kreider, a south-of-the-border twist by adding cinnamon and coffee. I prefer to leave the chopped nuts out of the pudding and serve them separately to sprinkle over the top. What could be better than a scoop of vanilla ice cream and crisp nuts atop the warm cake and fudge-y sauce? Oh, yum!

Favorite Family Supper

Penne with Eggplant, Tomatoes,
Fresh Mozzarella, and Herbs

Simple Sautéed Pecans over
Ice Cream with Liqueur Drizzle

THIS FAMILY FAVORITE *combines the rich, gooey, addictive quality of a baked eggplant Parmesan casserole with the freshness of ripe tomatoes, herbs, and chewy pasta. Plus, it is quick and easy to put together on top of the stove – no oven heat needed - making this a great summer menu.*

Penne with Eggplant, Tomatoes, Fresh Mozzarella, and Herbs

Serves 6-8 • *Prep. Time: 20 minutes* • *Cooking Time: 30 minutes*

3 eggs

¼ cup flour

½ tsp. salt

¼ tsp. pepper

6 cups peeled, 1" cubes eggplant

½ cup olive oil, *divided*

1 lb. penne, or other chunky pasta

1 pint cherry, or grape, tomatoes, halved

4 large garlic cloves, minced

1 cup chopped fresh parsley

¼ tsp. crushed red pepper flakes, or more to taste

12 oz. fresh mozzarella, cut into 1" cubes

½ cup grated Parmesan cheese

6 large, fresh basil leaves, torn into bite-size pieces

salt and freshly ground pepper, to taste

freshly grated Pecorino, or Parmesan, cheese

1. Bring a large covered pot of salted water to a boil.

2. Meanwhile, in a large mixing bowl, beat the eggs. Whisk in the flour, salt, and pepper.

3. Add the eggplant cubes and toss to coat.

4. Heat ¼ cup of the olive oil in a large skillet until the oil is hot, but not smoking.

5. Fry half the eggplant cubes over medium heat for about 8 minutes, turning to brown lightly on all sides.

6. Remove the browned eggplant with a slotted spoon. Drain on paper towels.

7. Add 2 Tbsp. olive oil to the skillet and continue frying the second batch of eggplant cubes. Remove from skillet, sprinkle with salt, and set aside.

8. Cook the pasta in the boiling water until al dente. Drain.

9. While the pasta cooks, heat the remaining 2 Tbsp. of oil in a large saucepan. Add the tomatoes, garlic, parsley, and red pepper flakes. Sauté 2-3 minutes, stirring gently.

10. Combine the pasta, mozzarella cubes, eggplant, and tomato mixture. Serve immediately, passing additional grated cheese at the table.

Simple Sautéed Pecans over Ice Cream with Liqueur Drizzle

Serves 6-8 • *Prep. Time: 5 minutes* • *Cooking Time: 5-7 minutes*

2 Tbsp. butter

2 cups pecan halves, or coarsely chopped pecans

1 tsp. sugar

dash of salt

Amaretto, or coffee liqueur, to taste

vanilla ice cream

1. Melt butter in skillet. Add pecans.

2. Stir and sauté over medium high heat until fragrant. Remove from heat.

3. Sprinkle with sugar and salt. Stir.

4. Serve over vanilla ice cream with a drizzle of liqueur.

The family on their deck in Puerto Rico, 1979. Nelson has been added to the clan. From left to right: Esther Rose, Steven, Susan, Ron, Jane, Nelson, Ellen, Sibyl, Ann.

Homemade Coffee Liqueur

Makes 4 cups • *Prep. Time: 5 minutes* • *Cooling Time: 1 hour* • *Standing Time: 3 weeks*

2 cups water

3 cups sugar

¾ cup instant
coffee granules
(decaf is fine)

2 cups vodka

1 or 2 vanilla beans

1. Bring 2 cups water to boil in a heavy medium saucepan.

2. Add sugar and coffee granules. Reduce heat to very low.

3. Stir just until sugar and coffee dissolve.

4. Remove from heat and let stand until cool, about 1 hour.

5. Add vodka. Pour into a large jar.

6. Split vanilla beans lengthwise. Scrape seeds from vanilla bean halves into the jar. Add the bean halves and stir to blend.

7. Cover the jar and let stand at room temperature for at least 3 weeks and up to 6 weeks. Discard vanilla bean halves before serving.

IN A BLIND
TASTE TEST,
*family members
chose this over
a familiar name
brand liqueur!*

THIS SIMPLE DESSERT *has always been a family favorite. We often served it with a pure maple syrup drizzle for the children, instead of the liqueur. Quick and easy, it's elegant enough for a company dinner.*

Favorite Guest Dinner

Fruity Salsa with Pita Crisps

Spicy Shrimp and Sausage
with Cheesy Grits

Spinach Salad with Mushrooms,
Croutons, and Warm Lemon Dressing

Rustic Italian Bread (see page 12)

Fresh Peach Galette

Fruity Salsa

Serves 6-8 • Prep. Time: 15 minutes

2 mangoes, peeled and finely diced

¾ cup finely chopped red onion

½ cup chopped fresh cilantro

4 Tbsp. fresh lime juice

1 Tbsp. brown sugar

1 jalapeño pepper, seeded and
minced, *optional*

3 Tbsp. fresh ginger root,
finely minced or grated

freshly ground pepper, to taste

salt, to taste

1. Combine all ingredients in a
   bowl and toss gently to mix.

2. Serve with Pita Crisps
   (see below), and/or crackers
   and tortilla chips.

Pita Crisps

Serves 6 • Prep. Time: 10 minutes • Broiling Time: 3-5 minutes

4 pita breads

3 Tbsp. sesame seeds

3 Tbsp. fresh thyme leaves

3 Tbsp. poppy seeds

⅔ cup olive oil

salt and black pepper,
to taste

1. Split the pitas in half.

2. Crush the sesame seeds, thyme, and poppy seeds
   together in a mortar to release their flavors.

3. In a small bowl, stir together the olive oil and
   crushed herbs and seeds.

4. Brush the mixture over the cut sides of the
   pitas. Broil until golden and crisp, 3-6 minutes.
   Alternatively, grill the pitas. Cool.

5. When cooled, break them into pieces and serve.
   Store extra crisps in a sealed container. These
   keep well and go wonderfully with any dips.

Spicy Shrimp and Sausage with Cheesy Grits

Serves 8 • *Prep. Time: 25 minutes* • *Cooking Time: 35-45 minutes*

THE GRITS

4 cups milk

2 cups water

2 Tbsp. butter

1 tsp. salt

¼ tsp. freshly ground black pepper

1½ cups quick-cooking grits

½ cup grated fontina cheese

½ cup grated cheddar cheese

hot pepper sauce, *optional*

1. Bring milk, water, butter, salt, and pepper to a boil in a medium non-stick saucepan.

2. Stir in the grits over low heat.

3. Cover and cook for 10 minutes, stirring occasionally.

4. Turn off the heat. Add the fontina and cheddar cheeses. Taste and add optional pepper sauce. Cover and keep warm.

WE ALL *look forward to this dish. When our families get together for vacation, someone always asks, "Is Sibyl going to make her Cheesy Grits?"*

Spicy Shrimp and Sausage with Cheesy Grits, continued

THE SAUSAGE AND SHRIMP

1½ lbs. raw shrimp, peeled and deveined

1 tsp. Creole seasoning

2 Tbsp. olive oil

1 lb. hot Italian sausage in casing

¼ lb. chorizo, *optional*

2 tsp. minced garlic, about 4 cloves

1½ cups chopped onion

2-3 roasted red bell peppers, chopped

2 cups chopped tomatoes, or 15-oz. can chopped tomatoes

⅓ cup red wine

1 tsp. sugar

¼ cup chopped fresh parsley

2 scallions, chopped, for garnish

1. Toss shrimp in Creole seasoning. Set aside.

2. Heat oil in a large skillet over medium heat. Add sausage. Brown and remove from skillet.

3. Slice the sausage and return to the skillet to brown further.

4. Add the chorizo and brown.

5. Add chopped garlic and onions. Cook, stirring for several minutes.

6. Stir in the roasted red peppers and diced tomatoes.

7. Stir in the wine, sugar, and parsley. Simmer for about three minutes.

8. Add the shrimp. Cook a few minutes, only until the shrimp turn pink. Add salt to taste.

COOK'S NOTE
If you want to roast your own peppers, see page 133.

TWO WAYS TO SERVE

1. Individually: Place grits in shallow bowls and ladle the shrimp and sausage mixture over top of each. Garnish with scallions and serve.

2. Mound the grits on a large, rimmed platter and ladle the shrimp and sausage around the sides. Or make a well in the center of the grits and ladle the shrimp and sausage in the middle. Garnish with scallions and serve.

Spinach Salad with Mushrooms, Croutons, and Warm Lemon Dressing

Serves 6-8 • *Prep. Time: 20 minutes* • *Cooking Time: 5-7 minutes*

1½ pounds fresh spinach, stemmed, washed, dried, and torn into pieces

½ lb. fresh cremini, or white, mushrooms, sliced thinly

⅓ cup extra-virgin olive oil

3 cups stale French, or Italian-style, bread, cut into ¾ inch cubes

¼ cup extra-virgin olive oil

2 medium cloves garlic, minced

¼ cup freshly squeezed lemon juice

salt and black pepper, to taste

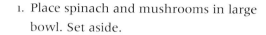

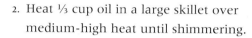

1. Place spinach and mushrooms in large bowl. Set aside.

2. Heat ⅓ cup oil in a large skillet over medium-high heat until shimmering.

3. Add the bread and fry, turning several times with slotted spoon, until crisp and golden, about 3 minutes. Transfer to paper-towel-lined plate.

4. Add the remaining ¼ cup olive oil to the skillet, along with the minced garlic.

5. Cook until lightly browned, about 2 minutes.

6. Whisk in the lemon juice and salt and pepper to taste. Cook and stir for a minute or two until warmed.

7. Pour warm dressing over spinach and mushrooms. Toss.

8. Add croutons. Toss again. Serve immediately.

Fresh Peach Galette

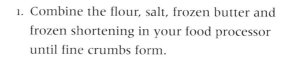

Serves 8 • *Prep. Time: 20 minutes* • *Baking Time: 40-45 minutes*

THE PASTRY

1½ cups flour

¼ tsp. salt

5 Tbsp. frozen butter

4 Tbsp. frozen vegetable shortening

4-5 Tbsp. ice water

1. Combine the flour, salt, frozen butter and frozen shortening in your food processor until fine crumbs form.

2. Add the ice water and process until mixture forms a ball.

3. Roll out between waxed paper to fit an 11"×13" casserole, plus an extra 2-3" to overlap the edges generously.

4. Lift into lightly greased casserole.

THE FILLING

7 large peaches, peeled and sliced

1 cup sugar

half stick (¼ cup) butter

1. Arrange the peaches over the crust in the bottom of the casserole.

2. Sprinkle the sugar over the peaches.

3. Bring the edges of the pastry up over the peaches and dot with the butter. The edges of the pastry will not cover the peaches. A messy look is good!

4. Preheat the oven to 450°, but when you put the galette in the oven, turn it down to 400°.

5. Bake for 40-45 minutes, or until the filling is bubbly and the crust is browned.

COOK'S NOTE
Sibyl sometimes makes this with a combination of blackberries and peaches, with delicious results!

CHAPTER 5

Ann Graber Miller

ANN, IDENTICAL TWIN with Sibyl, shares her talent as an artist. Although she has a master's degree in graphic design, she fell in love with watercolor, producing a collection of lush, colorful paintings before she turned her attention to her next love, interior and architectural design. Her unique talent is arranging rooms, using the belongings and collections of her clients to showcase their interests and personalities.

Ann has traveled and lived abroad extensively with her husband, Keith, a college professor, and their three children, Niles, Mia, and Simon. They spent many years overseas as leaders of student groups from Goshen College. Countries where they have taken student groups for multiple semester-long programs include Dominican Republic, Cuba, Costa Rica, Cambodia, and China. As they travel, they collect art objects from around the world, which they showcase in "Found," their gallery located in their hometown of Goshen, Indiana. Their most recent professional travels were in Southeast Asia, and Ann's Cambodian feast (page 103) is included in our collection of recipes.

Favorite Soup Supper

Annie's Carrot Soup

Whole Wheat Bread

Simple Salad with
Blender Vinaigrette

or

Shrimp and Kiwi Salad
(include this if guests are present)

Bob's Hot Fudge Sauce
over Vanilla Ice Cream

———————— ❧ ————————

THIS IS A GREAT SUPPER *menu we often enjoy.*
To turn this into a meal for company, you might
serve Shrimp Kiwi Salad, and add toasted pecans
or walnuts to the dessert tray.

Annie's Carrot Soup

Serves 6-8 • *Prep. Time: 15 minutes* • *Cooking Time: 30 minutes*

8-9 medium carrots, scrubbed and sliced

1 stick (½ cup) butter

2 Tbsp. sugar

4 Tbsp. flour

1-3 tsp. curry powder, depending on your taste for spice

6 cups chicken, or beef, broth

4 Tbsp. white wine, *optional*

salt and pepper, to taste

sour cream, or plain yogurt

1. In a large saucepan, sauté the sliced carrots in butter.

2. Sprinkle in sugar, flour, and curry powder.

3. Stir together for a few minutes.

4. Add broth and bring to a boil.

5. Continue to cook until carrots are tender.

6. Remove from heat. Purée in batches in your blender until smooth and silky, or directly in the pot with a stick blender.

7. Return to kettle. Add the white wine, if you wish, and gently reheat without boiling. Add salt and black pepper to taste.

8. Serve with dollops of sour cream or plain yogurt on top of each bowl.

THIS IS A GOOD SOUP *to have in your repertoire, as the ingredients are readily available, and the result is a rich, hearty, and satisfying meal.*

Whole Wheat Bread
(for a bread making machine)

Makes 1 2-lb. loaf • Prep. Time: 5 minutes • Rising Time: 2 hours 10 minutes • Baking Time: 28-30 minutes

1½ cups water

1½ tsp. salt

1½ Tbsp. vegetable oil

2 Tbsp. molasses

2 cups bread flour

2 cups whole wheat flour

2 tsp. active dry yeast

1. Measure all ingredients into bread machine in given order.

2. Set bread machine to "dough" setting (1 hour 30 min.).

3. Remove dough from machine and shape into a loaf.

4. Place in a greased 9" × 5" loaf pan. Let rise 40 minutes.

5. Bake at 350° for 28-30 minutes.

Blender Vinaigrette

1 cup • *Prep. Time: 5 minutes*

¼ cup cider vinegar

1 small onion, coarsely chopped

½ tsp. salt

¼ cup sugar

¾ cup vegetable oil

1. Place all in a blender and process until very smooth.

2. Taste and adjust seasonings.

THIS IS *one of those recipes that invites endless variations on the basic theme. We sometimes add Dijon mustard or curry powder, vary the amount of sugar or leave it out altogether, and sometimes toss in some parsley or fresh cilantro for a lovely green color and a distinct flavor. You may halve the vinegar and add 2 Tbsp. fresh lime or lemon juice.*

WHEN PUTTING TOGETHER *your salad, keep it simple and colorful. Tear the lettuce leaves into a shallow serving dish. Add tomatoes, slices of bell peppers, black olives, green onions, and mozzarella cubes, for instance. Your favorite combination of greens and veggies, with this fresh dressing, will make a perfect accompaniment for a hearty soup supper.*

For an Avocado Salad, simply slice a ripe avocado onto a pretty plate with a bed of greens. Sprinkle with snipped cilantro, and drizzle with the Blender Vinaigrette. This salad goes particularly well with the Puerto Rican dinner on page 160.

Shrimp and Kiwi Salad

Serves 6 • *Prep. Time: 15 minutes* • *Cooking Time: 3-5 minutes*

1 tsp. olive oil

¾ lb. medium-to-large peeled
and deveined raw shrimp,
about 24-30 shrimp

1 Tbsp. olive oil

2 Tbsp. chopped green onions

2 Tbsp. chopped fresh cilantro

2 Tbsp. rice vinegar

2 Tbsp. fresh lime juice

1 tsp. grated lime rind

⅛ tsp. salt

⅛ tsp. black pepper

4-6 cups torn red lettuce leaves

1½ cups peeled, cubed
kiwi, about 3 kiwi

1. Heat 1 tsp. oil in a large non-stick
   skillet over medium-high heat.

2. Add shrimp. Sauté 3-4 minutes, or just
   until shrimp turn white and are tinged
   with pink. Set aside to cool slightly to
   serve them at room temperature.

3. In a medium bowl combine the 1 Tbsp.
   oil, green onions, cilantro, rice vinegar,
   lime juice, lime rind, salt, and pepper.

4. Add shrimp. Toss to coat.

5. Divide lettuce among 6 individual
   salad plates. Divide the shrimp and
   dressing mixture among them. Finish
   by topping with the kiwi. Alternatively,
   arrange the salad on a large platter.

TO TURN *your
soup supper into
a company meal,
consider serving
this delicious salad.*

Bob's Hot Fudge Sauce over Vanilla Ice Cream

1 cup • *Prep. Time: 5 minutes* • *Cooking Time: 10 minutes*

2 oz. dark, unsweetened chocolate

half stick (4 Tbsp.) butter

¼ cup unsweetened cocoa powder

¾ cup sugar

¾ cup evaporated milk

dash salt

1 tsp. vanilla

1. In a double boiler over simmering water, melt the chocolate and butter.

2. Off heat add the cocoa powder. Blend well.

3. Add the sugar, milk, and salt.

4. Place mixture in pan over direct heat. Slowly bring to a boil, stirring constantly.

5. Boil until smooth and slightly thickened. Remove from the heat and stir in the vanilla.

6. Beat well with a whisk or a wooden spoon for 2 minutes.

7. Serve warm over ice cream. Store any extra in the refrigerator after it is completely cooled.

WE WERE SO LUCKY *to meet Bob, Steve and Yvonne's neighbor, who had retired from his profession as chief pastry chef at Nieman Marcus and published his own dessert cookbook. Our favorite chocolate sauce recipe comes from Bob. We're sharing it here with his blessing. This sauce keeps well in the refrigerator, so just go ahead and double the recipe!*

Favorite Family Supper

Khmer Chicken Curry

Cucumber Salad

Jasmine Rice (see page 172)

Wonton Banana Fritters

DAUGHTER ANN'S FAMILY *has been fortunate to live in Cambodia for two five-month periods, both times while working with Goshen College's international education program. Thai food has been a lifelong favorite of Ann's, even before she was able to go to this part of the world, so she was thrilled to travel to neighboring Thailand for 10 days on her most recent Cambodian sojourn. Others of us in the family love Southeast Asian cooking, too, and we seek it out even when we're traveling in the United States.*

Ann's recipes here, which we have eaten often in her home and at family gatherings, consist of some of her Cambodian favorites. Once when Ann and her husband were doing a public lecture on the history and culture of Cambodia, a professional cook expanded these recipes to serve 200 people! The cook liked the recipe so well she made it one of her regular offerings for catered meals.

ONE OF THE GREAT *things about curries is that you can prepare them a day in advance and allow the spices to blend. That makes for a richer curry and also allows for more focused time preparing other fresh dishes just before guests arrive.*

Khmer Chicken Curry

Serves 8-10 • *Prep. Time: 20 minutes* • *Cooking Time: 40-60 minutes*

1 large onion, diced

1 Tbsp. oil

3 tsp. ground coriander

1 Tbsp. curry powder

2 tsp. turmeric

2 large cloves garlic, minced

4 cups coconut milk

4 cups chicken broth

2 cups fresh green beans, sliced diagonally

4-6 medium potatoes, peeled and diced

4 cups canned tomatoes, diced

3 Tbsp. fish sauce

3 Tbsp. dark brown sugar

3 Tbsp. fresh lime juice

6 Kaffir lime leaves, or 1 tsp. lime zest

1-2 tsp. red pepper flakes, to taste

4 boneless, skinless chicken breast halves, sliced thinly

snipped cilantro, to garnish

1. In a large pot, sauté the onion in oil until transparent.

2. Add coriander, curry powder, turmeric, and garlic.

3. Add the coconut milk and chicken broth. Bring to a boil.

4. Stir in the beans, potatoes, tomatoes, fish sauce, brown sugar, lime juice, Kaffir lime leaves, and red pepper flakes.

5. Cook until potatoes are tender, 10-20 minutes.

6. Add the sliced chicken breasts. Cook just till chicken is cooked through, 2-3 minutes.

7. Taste for salt and sugar. Add more red pepper flakes if desired. Garnish with snipped cilantro to serve.

Cucumber Salad

Makes 4-6 cups • *Prep. Time: 15 minutes*

4 Tbsp. fish sauce

4 Tbsp. sugar

2 Tbsp. fresh lime juice

1 Tbsp. rice vinegar

4 garlic cloves, minced

red pepper flakes, to taste

⅓ cup hot water

1 medium carrot, shredded

2-3 cucumbers, peeled, seeded and
cut into sticks

½ cup chopped cilantro

1. Mix together fish sauce, sugar, lime juice, vinegar, garlic, red pepper flakes, and hot water. Chill. This mixture will keep in the refrigerator for up to 3 days.

2. To serve salad, pour dressing over carrot, cucumbers, and cilantro. Toss gently.

Before leaving Cambodia after a five-month stint in 2010, Ann's family went to a local photographer to have their photo taken as Cambodian families do. The photo studio provided the clothing, hair, makeup styling, and the jewelry.

Wonton Banana Fritters

Makes 24 fritters, serving 8 people with 3 fritters each • *Prep. Time: 30 minutes
Cooking Time: 20 minutes, depending on size of pan*

1 banana, finely chopped

½ tsp. cinnamon

¼ tsp. nutmeg

½ tsp. lime zest

1 tsp. lime juice

½ tsp. sugar

48 wonton wrappers

vegetable oil for deep frying

maple syrup to garnish

powdered sugar to garnish

1. Mix banana, cinnamon, nutmeg, lime zest, lime juice, and sugar together to make the filling.

2. Place a generously rounded teaspoonful of filling in the center of one wonton wrapper.

3. Moisten all 4 edges of the wonton with a little water on your fingertips. Top with another wonton wrapper, turning 45 degrees to form a star. Press edges together to seal completely. Set aside, but do not stack.

4. Pour oil to a depth of 2" in a heavy, deep saucepan. Heat to 325°-350°.

5. Put in a few fritters at a time without crowding the pan. Fry about 2 minutes until crispy and browned on both sides.

6. Drizzle with maple syrup. Sprinkle with powdered sugar.

COOK'S NOTE
Lovely served with ice cream and Bob's Hot Fudge Sauce (page 102).

Favorite Guest Dinner

Feta, Garlic, and Herb Dip

Baked Chicken Caribe

Yellow Rice Pilaf

Mediterranean Salad Platter with
Balsamic Vinaigrette

Rustic Italian Loaf
(see page 12)

Easy Chocolate Tiramisu Torte

Feta, Garlic, and Herb Dip

Makes about 3 cups • *Prep. Time: 10 minutes*

8 oz. feta cheese

12 oz. cream cheese, at room temperature

½ cup mayonnaise

6 dashes hot pepper sauce, or hot chili sauce

1 large garlic clove, finely minced

2 tsp. minced fresh basil,
or 1 tsp. dried basil

2 tsp. minced fresh dill,
or 1 tsp. dried dill weed

2 tsp. fresh thyme leaves,
or 1 tsp. dried thyme

freshly ground black pepper, to taste

sour cream, *optional*

1. Combine feta, cream cheese, and mayonnaise in a food processor. Blend well, scraping down the sides with a rubber spatula as needed.

2. Add the hot sauce, garlic, basil, dill, and thyme. Pulse briefly to blend. Add pepper to taste.

3. Add enough sour cream to make it the dipping consistency you want. To make a thick spread for crackers or pita crisps, omit the sour cream.

COOK'S NOTE
Serve this dip with crudités and assorted crackers.

THIS RECIPE INCLUDES *all the ingredients of a native Puerto Rican dish. In this case there is a lot of everything, and the result is absolutely delicious.*

You could put this together in the morning or early afternoon for several hours of marinating time and still have an excellent supper dish, but the extra overnight hours help the flavors penetrate the chicken for a superior result.

Baked Chicken Caribe

Serves 6-8 • *Prep. Time: 15 minutes* • *Marinating Time: 4-12 hours* • *Baking Time: 1-½ hours*

3-4 lbs. (8-10) boneless, skinless chicken thighs

½ tsp. salt

freshly ground black pepper, to taste

6 bay leaves

½ cup olive oil

½ cup red wine vinegar

½ cup green, pimento-stuffed olives

⅓ cup capers

¾ cup finely slivered prunes

3 Tbsp. dried oregano

8-10 cloves garlic, minced

½ cup brown sugar

1 cup white wine

¼-½ cup chopped, fresh cilantro

1. Season the chicken pieces with salt, and sprinkle with pepper.

2. Arrange the pieces in a single layer in a large, lightly greased, shallow glass or ceramic 10"×15" baking pan that you can bring to the table.

3. Distribute the bay leaves, olive oil, red wine vinegar, olives, capers, finely slivered prunes, oregano, and garlic over the chicken thighs.

4. Cover the pan tightly with plastic wrap. Refrigerate several hours or overnight.

5. Before baking, spread the brown sugar over the chicken. Pour the white wine over all.

6. Bake, uncovered, in a 350° oven until the chicken is tender, basting once or twice, one hour or more.

7. Just before serving, sprinkle generously with snipped cilantro.

Yellow Rice Pilaf

Serves 6-8 • *Prep. Time: 5 minutes* • *Cooking Time: 45 minutes*

2 Tbsp. butter

2 Tbsp. olive oil

1 small onion, chopped

1-2 cloves garlic, minced

¼ tsp. turmeric

½ tsp. curry powder

2 cups uncooked long-grain rice

3½ cups water

2 chicken bouillon cubes

salt and pepper, to taste

1. Heat the butter and oil in a large, heavy saucepan.

2. Add the chopped onion and the minced garlic.

3. Sauté for a few minutes until the onion is transparent.

4. Add the turmeric, curry powder, and rice. Continue sautéing, stirring constantly until rice grains become opaque, about 4 minutes.

5. Add water and bouillon cubes.

6. Bring to a boil, uncovered. Stir to dissolve bouillon cubes. Taste the broth for salt. Add salt and pepper to taste.

7. Reduce heat to low. Cover and cook until rice is tender, about 25 minutes.

8. Fluff the rice with a fork. If it is too dry and not quite tender, add a bit of water and cover, cooking again over low heat until tender.

Mediterranean Salad Platter

Serves 8 • *Prep. Time: 15 minutes* • *Cooking Time: 5 minutes*

1 lb. fresh green beans, trimmed

½ cup pine nuts

1 head romaine lettuce, torn into bite-size pieces

2 handfuls arugula, torn

1 large red onion, thinly sliced

2-3 medium tomatoes, cut into chunks

6-oz. jar marinated artichokes, chopped

6 oz. feta cheese, crumbled

5 small red potatoes, cooked, cooled, and quartered, *optional*

1. Blanch the green beans by dropping them into a pot of boiling, salted water for 2 minutes. Then drain them and run them under cold water for a few minutes. Set aside to cool completely.

2. Toast the pine nuts by dry-frying them in a hot, ungreased skillet, shaking the pan frequently, until they are golden brown. Set aside to cool.

3. Scatter romaine and arugula over a large serving platter.

4. Arrange remaining ingredients, plus the cooled green beans, over all, ending with the pine nuts.

5. Drizzle with the balsamic vinaigrette just before serving.

BALSAMIC VINAIGRETTE

2 Tbsp. balsamic vinegar

¼ tsp. salt

½ cup olive oil

2-3 Tbsp. blood-orange olive oil

Combine all the vinaigrette ingredients in a covered jar. Shake well, or whisk in a small bowl.

△ COOK'S NOTE

If you can't get blood-orange-flavored olive oil, add ¼ teaspoon lemon or orange zest to the vinaigrette.

Easy Chocolate Tiramisu Torte

Chilling Time: 2 hours • Prep. Time: 30 minutes
Baking Time: 20-30 minutes, depending on the cake mix directions

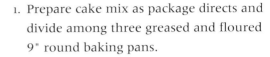

1 chocolate cake mix

¾ cup strong coffee (decaf is fine)

¼ cup coffee liqueur (see page 87
to make your own, if you wish)

1. Prepare cake mix as package directs and divide among three greased and floured 9" round baking pans.

2. Bake as directed, possibly shortening the baking time because of thinner layers. Cakes are done when a pick inserted in the middle comes out clean. Remove from pans and cool completely on wire racks.

3. When cooled, place each cake layer on a separate plate.

4. With a sharp tined fork, poke holes in each layer.

5. Combine ¾ cup coffee with ¼ cup coffee liqueur. Drizzle evenly over each layer. Set aside. Prepare filling and whipped cream.

FOR A *special occasion dessert, this tiramasu is hard to beat. It's based on a chocolate cake foundation instead of the traditional pudding and ladyfingers. Nobody will ever guess you started with a cake mix.*

Easy Chocolate Tiramisu Torte, continued

THE FILLING AND WHIPPED CREAM

8-oz. pkg. cream cheese, at room temperature

¾ cup powdered sugar, *divided*

5 Tbsp. coffee liqueur, *divided*

2 cups whipping cream

1. Place a medium bowl and beaters in the freezer to chill.

2. In large bowl combine cream cheese, ½ cup powdered sugar, and 3 tablespoons coffee liqueur. Beat until smooth. Set aside.

3. In the chilled bowl, combine whipping cream, ¼ cup powdered sugar, and 2 tablespoons coffee liqueur. Beat until stiff.

4. Fold half of the whipped-cream mixture into the cream-cheese mixture. Refrigerate the other half of the whipped cream mixture for final topping.

5. Spread half the cream-cheese/whipped-cream mixture over the bottom cake layer.

6. Top with the second cake layer. Spread the second cake layer with the remaining cream-cheese mixture.

7. Add the third cake layer.

8. Top with the reserved half of the whipped-cream mixture. Cover and chill thoroughly, at least 2 hours.

9. If desired, drizzle fudge sauce onto dessert plates before adding cake slices. Mix ¼ cup warmed fudge ice-cream topping (see Bob's Hot Fudge Sauce, page 102) with 2 Tbsp. coffee liqueur.

CHAPTER 6

Susan Graber Hunsberger

SUSAN, OUR YOUNGEST daughter, is also an artist. Her specialty is animal portraiture, featuring pets in their home settings painted in a style reminiscent of the Old Masters. She also does work in graphic design, interior decoration, photography, and illustration.

For more than a decade she lived in Bulgaria with her husband, Michael, a real estate developer, and their daughter, Evelyn. Recently the family moved to New Zealand to farm cattle and sheep and learn more about sustainable agriculture and farming practices.

While living in Bulgaria, Susan and her family were able to travel throughout the Balkans, as well as Turkey, Greece, and Italy, picking up recipes and inspiration along the way. Particularly important to her is the ages-old idea of cooking with local, seasonal ingredients. In her section she introduces us to a menu of typical Bulgarian dishes, all of which are easy to prepare, in spite of their difficult-to-pronounce names.

Finding fresh influences in her new home country, and a farmers market around every corner, Susan's guest menu features the local ingredients and culinary traditions of New Zealand.

Favorite Soup Supper

Sweet Potato & Coconut Soup
with **Shrimp** and **Snow Peas**

Honey-Lime Fruit with **Fresh Mint**

Sweet Potato & Coconut Soup with Shrimp and Snow Peas

Serves 6-8 • Prep. Time: 15 minutes • Cooking Time: 30 minutes

COOK'S NOTE

Red curry paste is available at most food stores in the Asian section or at the Asian market.

COOK'S NOTE

If snow peas are unavailable, substitute fresh asparagus, white or green, with its tough ends snapped off or peeled, and sliced in bite-sized pieces.

1 Tbsp. olive oil

1 Tbsp. Thai red curry paste

1 yellow onion, diced

1 clove garlic, minced

2 tsp. fresh ginger root, minced or grated

½ tsp. ground cumin

¼ tsp. cinnamon

1 tsp. packed brown sugar

2 lbs. sweet potatoes, peeled and cut into ½ inch dice, about 5 cups

4 cups chicken broth

2 cups unsweetened coconut milk

1 cup snow peas, or sugar snap peas, cut in half diagonally

2 cups raw shrimp, peeled, and cut in half

A handful of fresh cilantro, chopped, for garnish

1. Combine the oil, curry paste, onion, garlic, ginger root, spices, and sugar in a large kettle over medium heat.

2. Cook, stirring, until the onion is transparent, 6-8 minutes.

3. Add the sweet potatoes, chicken broth, and coconut milk.

4. Raise the heat to high and bring to a boil. As soon as it boils, cover, reduce the heat to simmer, and cook on low for 10 minutes, or until the sweet potatoes are tender. Don't overcook.

5. Taste for salt and adjust seasoning. You can prepare the soup ahead to this point.

6. About 5 minutes before serving, bring the soup back to a simmer.

7. Add snow peas and shrimp. Cook a few minutes, or just until the shrimp turn pink, but no longer! The peas will still be crisp and the shrimp perfectly tender.

8. Serve the soup in bowls with a generous sprinkling of cilantro.

PICTURE YOURSELF *on a Caribbean island when you eat this soup. The combination of coconut milk, fresh ginger, and spices, along with the sweet potatoes, tender shrimp, and crisp snow peas, is nothing short of a trip to tropical paradise!*

Honey Lime Fruit
with Fresh Mint

Serves 6-8 • *Prep. Time: 20 minutes*

2 Tbsp. lime juice

2-3 Tbsp. honey

5-7 mint leaves, washed, dried, very finely minced

5-6 cups assorted fruit - melon, grapes, bananas, oranges, kiwi, strawberries, mango, pineapple, etc.

Fresh mint leaves for garnish

1. In a small bowl combine the lime juice and the honey. Mix well. Check for balance, and adjust to your taste.

2. Add minced mint.

3. In a larger bowl combine the peeled, seeded, cubed, or sliced fruit.

4. Pour the honey/lime mixture over the fruit and toss gently to combine.

5. Serve in a pretty bowl, garnished with fresh mint leaves.

COOK'S NOTE

If limes are not available, substitute fresh lemon in the dressing, and try finely minced basil or lemon-thyme in place of the mint.

Favorite Family Supper

Grilled Italian Shrimp Skewers

Simple Lemon Pasta

Variation on a Capri Salad

Sticky Date Cake with
Balsamic Caramel Cream

THIS MENU TRIO *never fails to please: the crispy shrimp, the creamy pasta, and the salad made with garden herbs. It's a menu of minimum effort in the kitchen and maximum dining pleasure, special enough to impress guests. Serve it as a luncheon or dinner at a dressy table inside or outside on the patio. It's best made during the summer when your herb garden is productive and the cherry tomatoes can come straight off the vine.*

Grilled Italian Shrimp Skewers

Serves 4 • Prep. Time: 15 minutes • Standing Time: 30 minutes • Grilling/Broiling Time: 4 minutes

20 tiger prawns, or large shrimp, peeled and deveined

3 Tbsp. olive oil

½ cup fine, dry, bread crumbs or panko

1 clove garlic, finely minced

1-2 Tbsp. finely chopped fresh dill

¼ tsp. salt

¼ tsp. ground black pepper

1. Rinse the shrimp in cold water and pat dry.

2. Put them in a large bowl and add the oil, mixing them to coat evenly.

3. Add the remaining ingredients. Toss everything together to coat the shrimp evenly. Cover. Allow to sit for half an hour. (Can be prepared ahead of time to this point and kept in the refrigerator for several hours.)

4. Thread 5 shrimp per skewer, through the middle, including the tail ends so they don't swing around. Shake off excess crumbs.

5. Grill or broil for about 2 minutes on each side, or until the bread crumbs are golden. Don't overcook the shrimp. Make sure everything else on the menu is ready and family members are on standby!

COOK'S NOTE

If you don't serve these with Lemon Pasta, add 1 Tbsp. lemon zest to the crumb mixture.

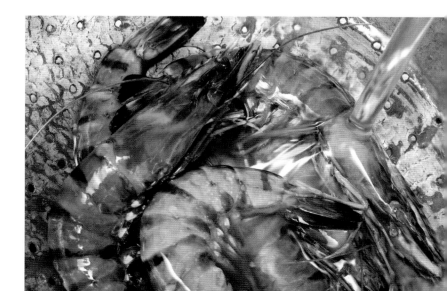

THIS CREAMY DISH is not made with heaps of cheese. It's the lemon juice reacting with the cream that thickens it, making this lemony sauce so simple, bright, and fresh.

Simple Lemon Pasta

CHAPTER 6

SUSAN'S
MENU

FAVORITE
FAMILY
SUPPER

Serves 4 • *Prep. Time: 15 minutes* • *Cooking Time: 10-15 minutes*

4 Tbsp. butter

½ cup whipping cream

½ cup milk

2 tsp. lemon zest

3 Tbsp. fresh lemon
juice, about 1 large
lemon

¼ -½ tsp. salt, to
taste

¼ -½ tsp. coarsely
ground black pepper,
to taste

1 lb. egg pappardelle
or fettuccine

1. Set the oven to 150°.

2. Put the butter, cream, milk, lemon zest, lemon juice, salt, and pepper into a large ceramic serving bowl— the same bowl that will go to the table.

3. Place the bowl in the pre-warmed oven. The idea is to melt the butter and warm the dish. Too much heat will curdle the mixture and it won't be creamy anymore.

4. While the bowl is warming, boil the pasta according to package directions in heavily salted water until it is al dente.

5. While the water is boiling, remove the bowl from the oven and whisk until the mixture is smooth and creamy. Put the bowl back in the oven to stay warm.

6. Drain the water from the pasta.

7. Toss the pasta into the warmed bowl. Stir gently until the noodles are evenly coated.

8. Add a fresh grating of lemon peel and a quick grind of black pepper to finish. Serve immediately. You could also grate fresh Parmesan cheese over top, but I find the cheese is not essential to the dish.

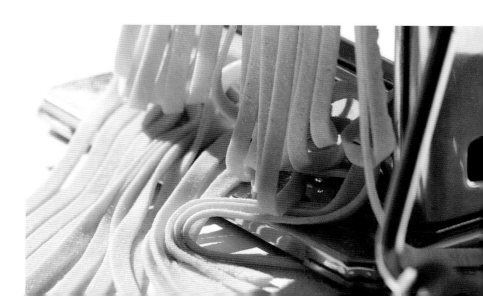

Variation on a Capri Salad

CHAPTER 6

SUSAN'S
MENU

FAVORITE
FAMILY
SUPPER

Serves 4 • Prep. Time: 15 minutes

20 cherry tomatoes, cut in half

generous drizzle extra-virgin olive oil

½-¾ tsp. salt, to taste

¼ cup fresh oregano leaves, or basil
leaves, roughly chopped

16 fresh mini mozzarella balls, or baby
bocconcini, drained and cut in halves

16 black kalamata olives, pitted

dash white balsamic vinegar

generous grind of black pepper

1. In a table-worthy serving bowl, place the tomatoes, olive oil, and salt together to mingle flavors.

2. Get the rest of the ingredients ready to toss into the bowl just before serving – herbs chopped, mozzarella drained and chopped, olives pitted. (I squish them with my thumb on a cutting board and rip out the pits.) The salad is best at room temperature, so these things can sit out on the counter while you prepare the pasta for this menu.

3. Right before serving, add the reserved ingredients to the bowl with the tomatoes. Give it a gentle toss and a very light dash of white balsamic vinegar.

THERE ARE MANY *subtle variations to the famous Caprese (or Capri-style) Salad. Because of the recipe's simplicity, success depends completely on fresh ingredients and high quality olive oil. The original doesn't call for vinegar, as it can break down the cheese, but a dash of white balsamic just before serving gives a refreshing note to the overall flavor. I could eat this all summer long.*

CHAPTER 6

SUSAN'S
MENU

FAVORITE
FAMILY
SUPPER

Sticky Date Cake with Balsamic Caramel Cream

Serves 4-6 • *Prep. Time: 30 minutes* • *Baking Time: 35-40 minutes*

2 cups pitted dates, roughly chopped

1½ cups water

1 tsp. baking soda

1 stick (½ cup) butter at room temperature

½ cup brown sugar

1 tsp. vanilla

2 eggs

2 cups all-purpose flour

1 tsp. baking powder

¼ tsp. salt

1. Combine dates and water in a small saucepan and bring to a boil.

2. Remove from heat and stir in baking soda. Set aside.

3. In a medium mixing bowl, cream the butter, sugar, and vanilla until light and fluffy.

4. Add eggs, one at a time, beating well after each.

5. Stir in the date mixture, the flour, baking powder, and salt. Mix until well combined.

6. Spoon the mixture into a greased and floured 9" springform pan.

7. Bake at 350° for 35-40 minutes, or until a skewer inserted into the center comes out clean. Let stand for 10 minutes on a cooling rack.

8. Carefully remove the sides of the pan. Slice and serve on individual plates topped with a generous amount of Balsamic Caramel Cream.

THIS CAKE IS RICH *and gooey with a wonderful date flavor, but it's the warm caramel sauce that will really leave you marveling. What sets it apart is the dash of balsamic vinegar, which you won't taste. It tempers the sweetness, gives it a tooth, and elevates this caramel sauce above the ordinary. If there's any cooled sauce left over, it's better than candy!*

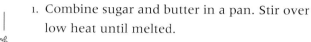

BALSAMIC CARAMEL CREAM

⅔ cup brown sugar

⅓ cup butter

½ cup heavy cream

3 tsp. balsamic vinegar

1. Combine sugar and butter in a pan. Stir over low heat until melted.

2. Whisk in the cream and vinegar. Bring to a boil, stirring occasionally.

3. Then turn off heat and whisk for 1 more minute.

4. Remove from heat and serve warm, not hot. As the sauce cools, it thickens to the perfect consistency for drizzling over the warm cake, and if refrigerated, it turns into a spreadable frosting.

Favorite Guest Dinner

Sun-Dried Tomato, Mint, and
Mascarpone Spread

Grilled, Spiced Lamb Chops

Roasted Yams (Kumara) and Garlic Cloves
with Sibyl's Roasted Red Pepper Sauce

Salad with Herbs and
Roasted Pumpkin Seeds

Mini Kiwi Pavlovas

———————— ⚘ ————————

Sun-Dried Tomato, Mint, and Mascarpone Dip

Makes 1½ cups • *Prep. Time: 5 minutes*

1 cup oil-packed, sun-dried tomatoes, drained of the oil

1 cup mascarpone

fresh mint leaves (I use 4 big sprigs)

¼ tsp. salt, or to taste

½ tsp. freshly ground black pepper

 COOK'S NOTE

Mascarpone cheese is slightly sweet, light, airy, and melts on your tongue. There's really no substitute, but in a pinch you can use cream cheese. It will be pretty thick, so add some milk to get a softer consistency.

1. Put the sun-dried tomatoes in a food processor and pulse until chopped coarsely.

2. Add all the other ingredients and pulse until mixed but not puréed. The herbs should be visible as little pieces.

3. Serve at room temperature.

THE NOTE *from Susan read: "I just served this to guests last night – they went nuts over it! I served it with crusty baguette slices, but crackers or breadsticks are good, too. When a recipe is this easy and gets devoured, we like to share the pleasure!"*

So you've just spent *a small fortune on lamb chops for your special dinner. All they need now is a quick spice rub to enhance their naturally delicious flavor, and straight onto the grill they go. These pair up nicely with the spicy smoky sweetness of Sibyl's Roasted Red Pepper Sauce on page 133.*

Grilled, Spiced Lamb Chops

Serves 6 • Prep. Time: 15 minutes • Grilling Time: 6-10 minutes

12-18 rib lamb chops

1 bunch lemon thyme, woody stems discarded, leaves chopped

3 cloves of garlic, chopped

1½ tsp. ground cumin

Salt and coarsely ground black pepper, to taste

olive oil

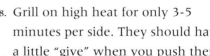

COOK'S NOTE

For better tasting spice, try roasting 1½ teaspoons cumin seeds on the stove until aromatic (shake the hot skillet back and forth until just smoking). Let them cool slightly, and then give them a quick whirl in a spice grinder.

1. Preheat the grill to high.

2. Chop the fresh thyme and garlic and make a little pile.

3. Add the cumin and toss the pile with your fingers.

4. Arrange the chops in a single layer on a tray. Salt and pepper them on both sides.

5. Dip each chop in the herb mixture and press the herbs into the meat.

6. Drizzle the chops with olive oil, and touch each chop to be sure it is coated nicely.

7. If everything else in your meal is prepared, then it's time to grill. If not, pop the chops into the fridge, covered, until you're ready.

8. Grill on high heat for only 3-5 minutes per side. They should have a little "give" when you push them with your finger.

CHAPTER 6

SUSAN'S
MENU

FAVORITE
GUEST
DINNER

Roasted Yams (*Kumara*) and Garlic Cloves

Serves 6-8 • *Prep. Time: 10 minutes* • *Baking Time: 30 minutes*

3 lbs. yams (or kumara), peeled and chopped in 2" pieces

1 head garlic, cloves separated, peeled and left whole

1 tsp. salt

½ tsp. freshly ground black pepper

¼ cup olive oil

¼ -½ cup water

handful of chopped fresh herbs, such as parsley, basil, or cilantro, *optional*

¼ cup crumbled feta, or goat cheese, *optional*

1. Combine the chopped yams and garlic cloves in a large roasting pan.

2. Sprinkle with salt, pepper, and olive oil. Toss to distribute evenly.

3. Add ¼ cup water and shake the pan.

4. Roast in center of oven at 375° for about 30 minutes, stirring occasionally, until soft and caramelized. You might need to add a bit more water to keep things from burning or sticking during this process.

5. Just before serving, gently stir in the optional chopped fresh herbs and crumbled goat cheese. Serve with Sibyl's Red Pepper Sauce, which you can make ahead and then reheat.

THE FIRST PEOPLE *of New Zealand, the Maori, ate a type of yam called* kumara, *which is used extensively in New Zealand cuisine, often combined with potatoes and mashed as a side dish. Here it is roasted with a bit of liquid, making creamy, caramelized pieces. The garlic cloves, left whole, impart their strength overall, but retain their own identity, so when you find them on your plate, softened and mellowed, they are little treats. For a change, add peeled and chopped potatoes to the dish and prepare in the same way.*

Sibyl's Roasted Red Pepper Sauce

CHAPTER 6

SUSAN'S
MENU

FAVORITE
GUEST
DINNER

Makes 2-3 cups sauce • Prep Time: 10 minutes
Roasting Time: 10 minutes • Standing Time: 15 minutes

4 Tbsp. olive oil

1 cup chopped onion, about
1 medium onion

2 garlic cloves, chopped

1 Tbsp. cumin seeds

½-1 red jalapeño pepper,
seeded and chopped

2 Tbsp. lime juice

4 red bell peppers, roasted,
then skinned and chopped
(see directions below)

1 Tbsp. molasses, or
dark brown sugar

¼ cup fresh parsley

salt and pepper, to taste

1. In a skillet, sauté onion and garlic in the olive oil until tender.

2. Add the cumin and jalapeño. Continue to cook for about a minute.

3. Add the lime juice. Simmer until sauce is reduced by half.

4. Transfer to a blender along with the chopped red pepper and the molasses.

5. Process until smooth, holding lid ajar to let any steam escape.

6. Season to taste, then blend in the parsley briefly.

TO ROAST THE RED PEPPERS

1. Cut the peppers in half. Discard seeds and membranes.

2. Place skin sides up on a foil-lined baking sheet. Flatten with your hands.

3. Broil for 10 minutes, or until well-blackened.

4. Remove from the broiler, wrap the blackened peppers in the foil, and let them steam for 15 minutes.

5. Open the foil, remove the peppers and pull off the blackened skin, leaving a bit of the charred part for extra flavor and color.

THE SIMPLE CLEAN FLAVORS *of this salad refresh the palate when served alongside a rich main dish such as grilled lamb.*

Salad with Herbs and Roasted Pumpkin Seeds

Serves 8 • *Prep: 25 minutes*

SALAD

7 generous cups mixed salad greens

3 generous cups mixed fresh herbs such as parsley, basil, cilantro, arugula, and chervil

⅓ cup hulled pumpkin seeds (also known as pepitas or pips)

⅓ cup hulled sunflower seeds

DRESSING

2 Tbsp. balsamic vinegar

1 tsp. Dijon mustard

½ tsp. salt, or to taste

¼ tsp. finely ground black pepper, or to taste

⅓ cup extra-virgin olive oil

1. Tear the salad leaves and the herbs into large pieces. Place in large serving bowl.

2. In an ungreased frying pan, dry-roast the seeds over medium high heat until golden, about 3 minutes. Toss them frequently so they don't burn. You should hear some popping noises as the pumpkin seeds puff. Set them aside to cool in the pan.

3. Combine all the dressing ingredients except the olive oil in a medium bowl.

4. Slowly pour the oil into the bowl, whisking continuously to emulsify the mixture. It should thicken slightly.

5. Taste and add more salt and pepper if needed.

6. Drizzle part of the dressing over the greens and toss gently with your fingers to coat the leaves lightly. Taste. You want to keep it light, so you may not need to use all the dressing.

7. Sprinkle the seeds on top and serve.

PAVLOVA, *the national dessert of both Australia and New Zealand, is a lovely, light presentation composed of a meringue base, Chantilly cream, and fresh fruits. Here the meringue is baked in individual-sized portions, the Chantilly cream is enhanced with vanilla bean seeds, the fruits are a gorgeous combination of bright green kiwi and dark blueberries, and the whole thing is finished off with a simple strawberry coulis.*

Another beautiful thing about this dessert is that all the components can be prepared in advance. Assemble just before serving to keep the meringue cups crisp.

CHAPTER 6

SUSAN'S
MENU

FAVORITE
GUEST
DINNER

Mini Kiwi Pavlovas

Serves 8 • *Prep. Time: 25 minutes* • *Baking Time: 45-55 minutes* • *Cooling Time: 30 minutes*

4 egg whites, room
temperature

1¼ cups sugar, *divided*

¼ tsp. cream of tartar,
or ½ tsp. distilled
white vinegar, or
lemon juice

¼ tsp. salt

1 tsp. powdered sugar

1½ cups heavy cream

¼ tsp. vanilla bean paste,
or ½ tsp. vanilla

4 ripe but firm kiwis,
each peeled and
cut into 8 wedges

2 cups fresh blueberries,
or blackberries

3 cups strawberries,
hulled

1-2 Tbsp. sugar

1. Using an electric mixer, beat egg whites in large bowl until soft peaks form.

2. Gradually add 1 cup sugar, beating continuously until the mixture resembles marshmallow cream, about 4 minutes.

3. Beat in the cream of tartar (or vinegar or lemon juice), salt, and powdered sugar.

4. Drop meringue onto a large, parchment-paper-lined baking sheet in 8 mounds, spacing apart. Bear in mind that the meringue will expand during baking.

5. Using a spoon, make an indentation in the center of each to form a shallow cup.

6. Place in 350° oven and immediately reduce temperature to 250°.

7. Bake until meringues are dry outside but centers are still soft, 45-55 minutes.

8. Turn off the oven, open the door, and leave them to cool on the rack for at least 30 minutes.

9. For the Chantilly Cream: use an electric mixer to beat cream with ¼ cup sugar and vanilla paste in a medium bowl until peaks form. Cover and set aside, or refrigerate if assembling later.

10. For the Strawberry Coulis: use a stick blender to purée strawberries and 1-2 Tbsp. sugar together until completely smooth.

11. To assemble the dessert, peel the meringues off the parchment paper and place on individual dessert plates.

12. Spoon Chantilly cream into each.

13. Arrange kiwi wedges and berries on top.

14. Spoon strawberry coulis around outside of plate and drizzle some over fruit. Serve immediately.

CHAPTER 7

Yvonne Schussler Graber

Yvonne, who married our son, Steven, our sixth and last child, was born in what was then West Germany. Her childhood in Germany was filled with daily bicycle trips with her grandmother to the market, where together they chose ingredients for meals that were simple, fresh, and hearty. Later, Yvonne moved to the United States with her mother and met Steven while completing her studies at Arizona State University.

It was at the Graber get-togethers where Yvonne first noticed the family's unusual focus on food and the bonding effects it can have. Determined to have that in her own home, Yvonne taught herself to cook. Steve and Yvonne entertain regularly and have gained a reputation for putting on fabulous outdoor dinner parties.

Yvonne and Steven, along with their children, Jacob and Sarah, live in Scottsdale, Arizona. Steve designs and builds custom cars for street and track through his Graber Cars business (www.grabercars.com), and Yvonne is an intensive care nurse. The flavorful Spanish, Native American, and Mexican cooking of the area inspired Yvonne's recipes in this section of the cookbook. Her menus are considerably more spicy than her grandmother's, but still simple, fresh, and hearty.

Favorite Soup Supper

Chili Con Carne

Cheese Quesadillas

Lettuce Wedge with Ranch Dressing
(recipe not included)

Fried Ice Cream

We use this family-favorite chili recipe every year for Jane's open house. For the open house we make it (x5!) weeks ahead of time and freeze it, leaving out the beans, which are added the morning of the party. Our secret final ingredient is hickory-smoked barbecue sauce. You can use a different brand than our favorite, but be sure it's hickory-smoked for that good, smoky flavor.

When the chili is served for a family meal, have optional garnishes available to serve alongside: grated cheddar or Jack cheese, freshly chopped cilantro, chopped green onions, and sour cream.

Chili Con Carne

Serves 8 • Prep. Time: 15 minutes • Cooking Time: 1 hour

1 lb. ground beef

1 lb. ground turkey

½ lb. smoked sausage, or kielbasa
(preferably skinless), diced

olive oil

3 medium onions, chopped

1 green bell pepper, chopped

6 cloves garlic, minced, or
3 Tbsp. from a jar

2-3 Tbsp. chili powder

2 tsp. ground cumin

2 tsp. dried oregano

2 16-oz. cans chopped
tomatoes with juice

15-oz. can tomato sauce

1-2 tsp. sugar

3 bay leaves

1-2 tsp. salt, to taste

2 cups water

2-3 15-oz. cans pinto beans,
or chili beans, or a
combination of the two

2 Tbsp. Hunt's Hickory and
Brown Sugar Barbecue Sauce

1. In a large skillet crumble and cook the ground beef until browned. Remove with a slotted spoon to your soup kettle.

2. Now brown the turkey in the beef drippings. When cooked through, remove with the slotted spoon to the soup kettle.

3. Brown the diced sausage in the same skillet and remove to the soup kettle. Pour out and discard the drippings. By this time my skillet usually has lots of dark bits left from all that browning, so I clean it out and start fresh for the onions.

4. Sauté the onions, peppers, and garlic in a little olive oil over medium heat, stirring until vegetables are softened and the onions are a light golden.

5. Add the spices and continue stirring for 3-5 minutes. Add this mixture to your soup kettle.

6. Pour the tomatoes and the tomato sauce into the soup kettle. Add the sugar, the bay leaves, the salt, and the 2 cups of water. Bring to a boil.

7. Reduce heat. Cover and simmer for about 35 minutes. Taste and adjust seasonings.

8. At this point, you can set the chili aside to chill and freeze for later use, or continue by stirring in the quantity of beans you like.

9. Heat thoroughly. Add more water if you want a "soupier" chili.

10. Add secret ingredient—barbecue sauce— and taste. Adjust the seasonings. Taste again—mmm—and again!

Cheese Quesadillas

Serves 4 • Prep. Time: 5 minutes • Cooking Time: 15 minutes

4 12" flour tortillas

**2 cups shredded cheese,
your choice**

1. Heat a 12" skillet without oil.

2. Place ½ cup shredded cheese on half of each tortilla and fold over.

3. Place two at a time in the skillet and cook until light brown on the bottom.

4. Turn the quesadillas over and brown the other side. Serve hot.

WHAT COULD *be simpler? Quesadillas are the perfect accompaniment for chili, but they also make a delicious snack or appetizer. Serve them with salsa and sour cream for a quick lunch.*

Fried Ice Cream

Serves 4 • Prep. Time: 5 minutes • Freezing Time: 1 hour • Cooking Time: 5 minutes

4 balls vanilla ice cream, about 3" in diameter

4 cups crushed cornflakes

4 tsp. cinnamon

oil

whipped cream

honey

1. Combine crushed cornflakes and cinnamon.

2. Dredge ice cream balls in cornflake/cinnamon mixture until well-covered.

3. Place on a cookie sheet in your freezer until ready to serve, at least one hour.

4. Heat oil to 350°-400° in a deep fryer or a heavy saucepan with at least 3" of oil.

5. Place one ice cream ball at a time into oil for 6 seconds. Remove with a large slotted spoon.

6. Serve immediately with a dollop of whipped cream and a drizzle of honey.

Steve takes Mom (Esther Rose) for a spin in a La Bala, the car he designed and built.

143

Favorite Family Supper

Classic Mojitos

Cave Creek Carnitas

Warm Tortillas
(recipe not included)

Chunky Guacamole

Traditional Fresh Salsa
(see page 153)

Zesty Lime Cookies

———————— ❧ ————————

CHAPTER 7
YVONNE'S
MENU

FAVORITE
FAMILY
SUPPER

Classic Mojitos

Serves 2   •   Prep. Time: 5 minutes   •   Cooking Time: 5 minutes   •   Cooling Time: 1 hour

¼ cup sugar

¼ cup water

8 mint leaves

½ cup white rum

crushed ice

juice of one lime

½ cup club soda

lime wedges, for garnish

mint leaves, for garnish

1. Make simple syrup by putting sugar and water together in a saucepan. Bring to a boil, stirring to dissolve sugar. Remove from heat as soon as the syrup boils. Cool. Extra simple syrup stores in the refrigerator indefinitely.

2. To make 2 mojitos, place 1 Tbsp. simple syrup, 8 mint leaves, rum, ice, and lime juice into a shaker and shake vigorously.

3. Pour into two glasses and add club soda. Stir.

4. Add fresh lime wedges and a mint leaf to garnish.

YVONNE AND STEVEN were living in Cave Creek, Arizona, just north of Phoenix, when Yvonne perfected her recipe for carnitas.

You'll be getting more than one meal from this recipe. The leftover shredded pork is great as a filling for enchiladas, tacos, and wraps, as a topping for pizza, or even in an omelet.

COOK'S NOTE

An alternate cooking method, used by a test cook who didn't have a slow cooker, was to bake the ingredients in a tightly covered casserole at 250° for five hours.

After she shredded the pork, she puréed the broth with a stick blender. She said, "Broth yummy! No discarding allowed!" She returned the shredded meat to the broth and simmered it until most of the liquid was absorbed, about 1½ hours, with delicious results. Skipping the butter step kept the dish low-fat.

CHAPTER 7

YVONNE'S
MENU

FAVORITE
FAMILY
SUPPER

Cave Creek Carnitas

Serves 8 • Prep. Time: 10 minutes • Cooking Time: 8½ hours

2-3-lb. boneless pork shoulder

juice and zest of one lime

4 cloves garlic

2 chipotle whole chilies in adobo sauce
(freeze extras from a 4-oz. can)

1 Tbsp. powdered cumin

1 Tbsp. dried coriander

1 Tbsp. dried oregano

1 onion, quartered

3 cups chicken broth, or 1½ cubes
organic chicken bouillon
and 3 cups water

half stick (4 Tbsp.) butter

¼ cup orange juice

salt, to taste, depending on saltiness
of the chicken broth

flour tortillas

ACCOMPANIMENTS

salsa (bottled, or fresh, see page 153)

sour cream

diced tomato

shredded lettuce

fresh cilantro, chopped

lime wedges

chunky guacamole (see page 148)

1. Combine pork, lime juice and zest, garlic, chilies, cumin, coriander, oregano, onion, and broth in a large slow cooker. Cook on low for 8 hours, or until meat forks apart easily.

2. Remove the meat. Cool slightly, and tear or shred into bite-sized chunks. Discard the broth or save for another purpose.

3. In a large skillet, fry the meat in butter to brown some edges.

4. Add ¼ cup orange juice. Allow meat to absorb the juice for added flavor. Taste for salt and adjust as needed.

5. Serve with hot tortillas and your choice of accompaniments.

COOK'S NOTE

Yvonne usually buys the uncooked tortillas from the refrigerator section of the grocery store and follows the cooking directions on the package.

CHAPTER 7

YVONNE'S
MENU

FAVORITE
FAMILY
SUPPER

Chunky Guacamole

2 cups • *Prep. Time: 10 minutes*

2-3 ripe avocados, peeled and diced

1 Tbsp. finely chopped red onion

1 serrano chile pepper, minced

1 small tomato, seeded and diced

3 Tbsp. chopped cilantro

1-3 Tbsp. fresh lime juice

salt and pepper, to taste

COOK'S NOTE

You can substitute ¼ jalapeño, or 2-4 canned green chiles for the serrano chile.

1. Mix all with a fork, but not too much. Leave some texture.

2. Taste to adjust salt or lime juice. Serve.

CHAPTER 7

YVONNE'S
MENU

FAVORITE
FAMILY
SUPPER

Zesty Lime Cookies

Makes 2-3 dozen • *Prep. Time: 20 minutes* • *Chilling Time: 1-2 hours* • *Baking Time: 8-10 minutes*

2 sticks (1 cup) unsalted
butter, room temperature

1 cup granulated sugar

1 egg

5 tsp. grated lime zest

2 Tbsp. fresh lime juice

½ tsp. almond extract

1½ cups all-purpose flour

1 cup cornmeal

GLAZE

1½ cups powdered sugar

1½ tsp. lime zest

3-4 tsp. lime juice

1. Cream together the butter and sugar until fluffy.

2. Beat in the egg.

3. Add the lime zest, lime juice, and almond extract.

4. Stir in the flour and the cornmeal. Chill at least one hour.

5. Form 1" balls and place on greased cookie sheets.

6. Flatten slightly with a flat tumbler bottom dipped in cornmeal.

7. Bake at 350° for about 8-10 minutes. Let cool completely before drizzling with glaze.

8. Combine glaze ingredients in small bowl. Drizzle on cooled cookies.

THE SURPRISE INGREDIENT *in these cookies is the cornmeal. Who would have ever thought? It adds a subtle texture that's crisp, yet delicate.*

Yvonne likes to pair these with Mexican coffee: add a dash of coffee liqueur (see recipe on page 87) to a cup of coffee, and top with whipped cream.

149

Favorite Guest Dinner

Classic or **Strawberry Margarita**

Omi's Chiles Rellenos Dip
with Tortilla Chips

Traditional Fresh Salsa

Chicken Enchiladas
Enchiladas de Pollo

Refried Beans

Mexican Rice

Yvonne's Fudge Truffle Cheesecake

———————— ✳ ————————

Classic or Strawberry Margarita

Serves 4 • *Prep. Time: 10 minutes*

1 cup sweet and sour mix

½ cup triple sec, or Cointreau

½-1 cup tequila

6-oz. can frozen limeade concentrate

3 cups crushed ice, or more if you wish

1. Combine all the ingredients in a blender. Process until smooth.

2. Rim the glasses with salt, if desired.

STRAWBERRY MARGARITA

To turn this into a strawberry margarita, omit the limeade and substitute 1 cup frozen strawberries in syrup.

CHAPTER 7

YVONNE'S
MENU

FAVORITE
GUEST
DINNER

Omi's Chiles Rellenos Dip with Tortilla Chips

Serves 6-8 • *Prep. Time: 10 minutes* • *Baking Time: 1 hour*

1 cup half-and-half

2 eggs

⅓ cup flour

8 oz. Monterey Jack cheese,
shredded, *divided*

8 oz. cheddar cheese,
shredded, *divided*

4-oz. can diced green chiles

1 cup tomato sauce

tortilla chips

1. In a bowl, whisk together the half-and-half, eggs, and flour. Set aside.

2. In another bowl, mix the cheeses together.

3. Place half the cheese in a well-greased 9"×9" baking dish.

4. Top with the chiles, then the egg mixture.

5. Sprinkle remaining cheese on top. Pour the tomato sauce over top.

6. Bake uncovered for 1 hour at 350°.

7. Serve hot with tortilla chips for dipping.

YVONNE'S MOTHER, *Helma, is known to her Scottsdale grandchildren as "Omi," the German endearment for "Grandma." Omi lives nearby and has been an integral part of the children's lives since infancy.*

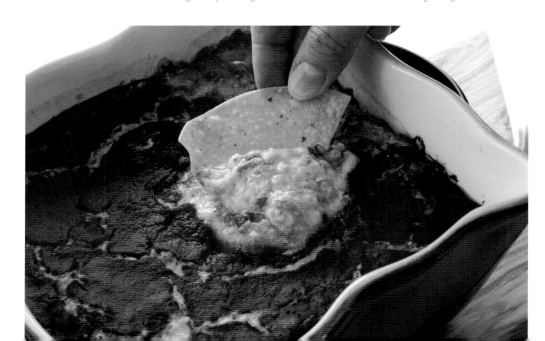

Traditional Fresh Salsa

CHAPTER 7

YVONNE'S
MENU

FAVORITE
GUEST
DINNER

2 cups • *Prep. Time: 15 minutes*

4-5 large, perfectly ripe tomatoes, quartered

1-2 sweet onions, such as Vidalia, in chunks

1-2 Tbsp. lime juice, about one lime

½-1 jalapeño pepper, seeded, chopped (Careful here. How hot do you want it?)

½-1 tsp. salt, or more to taste

1 tsp. minced garlic

1 cup fresh cilantro, or more – to your taste. We like quite a bit!

1. Place all the ingredients, starting with the lesser amounts listed, in your food processor. Process till coarsely chopped.

2. Taste. See if you want to add the larger amount of something now. Process briefly.

3. Serve with tortilla chips.

WHENEVER *we have a family party in the summertime, we get Yvonne to whip up her famous fresh salsa. Bring on the tortilla chips. This is as good as it gets.*

COOK'S NOTE

Leftover rotisserie chicken is perfect for this. Alternatively, boil one pound of boneless, skinless chicken breast in water to cover with 1 tsp. salt, 1 tsp. peppercorns, one bay leaf, and one small onion. Boil just until chicken is white through. Cool. Then shred or dice for the recipe opposite.

Chicken Enchiladas
Enchiladas de Pollo

Serves 6-8 • *Prep. Time: 30-40 minutes* • *Cooking Time: 45-50 minutes*

2 Tbsp. oil

1 onion, chopped

2 cups cooked chicken, diced or shredded

1 cup shredded Monterey Jack cheese

½ cup shredded sharp cheddar

½ cup salsa

¼ cup sour cream, or Mexican crema

12 corn tortillas

2 eggs

1 cup milk

¼ cup chopped cilantro, or more to your taste

½ tsp. salt

4-oz. can chopped green chilies

dash garlic powder

¼ tsp. cumin

shredded cheese, *optional*

1. To make the filling, sauté onion in oil in small skillet until translucent. Cool.

2. Combine chicken and onion in mixing bowl.

3. Add cheeses, salsa, and sour cream, Mix all together. Set aside.

4. Prepare the tortillas as per package instructions to soften for rolling.

5. Divide the chicken filling evenly between the 12 tortillas. Roll up.

6. Place seam-side down in a well-greased 9"×13" baking dish.

7. Prepare the enchilada sauce: beat the eggs in a medium mixing bowl.

8. Add milk, cilantro, salt, chilies, garlic powder, and cumin.

9. Pour enchilada sauce evenly over the rolled tortillas.

10. Bake at 350° for 45 minutes. If desired, top with extra shredded cheddar cheese and brown briefly under the broiler.

CHAPTER 7

YVONNE'S
MENU

FAVORITE
GUEST
DINNER

Refried Beans

Serves 6-8 • Prep. Time: 5 minutes • Soaking Time: 12 hours • Cooking Time: 2-3 hours

COOK'S NOTE
*Plan ahead for
this dish, since
you need to soak
the dried beans
overnight.*

2 cups dried beans, such as pinto

4 oz. fatty piece of bacon

1 bay leaf

3 Tbsp. lard, or oil

2 cloves garlic, minced

salt

1. Soak the beans overnight in a covered soup pot with a generous amount of water to cover.

2. Next morning, drain and rinse the beans. Add fresh water to cover.

3. Add bacon piece and bay leaf. Do not add salt. It will make the beans tough at this stage.

4. Boil the beans over medium-low heat for 2-3 hours, adding water as needed.

5. When the beans are tender, drain off the excess water.

6. In a saucepan heat the lard and add the garlic. Sauté gently 5 minutes.

7. Add the beans and fry, mashing some of them as they cook.

8. Add salt to taste.

*All of the Graber families
enjoy their pets—mostly dogs
and cats—although Sibyl's
farm also includes fainting
goats, horses, and chickens.*

Mexican Rice

CHAPTER 7

YVONNE'S
MENU

FAVORITE
GUEST
DINNER

Serves 4 • *Prep. Time: 5 minutes* • *Cooking Time: 40 minutes* • *Standing Time: 10 minutes*

¼ cup vegetable, or olive, oil

¼ onion, chopped

2 garlic cloves, minced

½ jalapeño pepper, minced

1 cup white long-grain rice

⅓ cup tomato paste

1 tsp. salt

2½ cups water

1. In a saucepan, heat oil and add onion, garlic, and jalapeño. Fry until onion is transparent, about 5 minutes.

2. Reduce heat and add rice. Fry 3 minutes, stirring constantly, until the rice is well-coated with the oil.

3. Stir in the tomato paste, salt, and water.

4. Bring to a boil and cover. Simmer on low heat for 30 minutes. Turn off heat.

5. Let stand, covered, for 10 minutes prior to serving.

ALL OF US *are such pushovers for cheesecake.*
Add chocolate and we fairly swoon with delight.
This recipe is an oft-repeated family favorite.

Yvonne's Fudge Truffle Cheesecake

Serves 12-16 • *Prep. Time: 20 minutes*
Cooking/Baking Time: 1 hour 15 minutes • *Chilling Time: 12 hours or overnight*

1½ cups vanilla wafer crumbs, about 45 wafers

½ cup powdered sugar

⅓ cup unsweetened cocoa powder

⅓ cup margarine, or butter, melted

3 8-oz. packages cream cheese, room temperature

14-oz. can sweetened condensed milk

12-oz. package semi-sweet chocolate chips

4 eggs

½ cup coffee flavored liqueur (see page 87)

2 tsp. vanilla

1. Prepare the crumb crust by combining the wafer crumbs, powdered sugar, cocoa powder, and butter.

2. Press mixture firmly in bottom and partly up sides of 9" springform pan.

3. Prepare the filling. In a large mixer bowl, beat the cream cheese until fluffy.

4. Gradually beat in the sweetened condensed milk until smooth.

5. Melt the chocolate in a small bowl in the microwave in 30-second increments, checking and stirring each time until completely melted. Beat the melted chocolate into the filling.

6. Add eggs, one at a time, beating well after each addition.

7. Stir in liqueur and vanilla. Blend well.

8. Pour into the prepared crust. Place a pan of water on the bottom oven rack to keep cheesecake from cracking.

9. Bake in a 300° oven for 1 hour and 5 minutes, or until center is set. Cool.

10. Chill overnight. Slice and serve.

The Puerto Rican Dinner

Puerto Rican Antipasto Platter

Pork Chops (*Chuletas*) a la Mrs. Comas

White Rice a la Caribe

Sofrito

Beans in Sauce (*Habichuelas Guisadas*)

Plantain Fritters or Fried Sweet Plantains
(*Tostones or Maduros*)

Caribbean Salad (*Ensalada Mixta*)

Pan de Agua or an Italian Loaf
(recipes not included)

Valetta's Coco Flan

Puerto Rican Antipasto Platter

1. Start your Puerto Rican party with an antipasto platter. Cube the following: guava paste, mild cheddar or longhorn cheese, summer sausage or salami, and fresh pineapple. Have ready pimento-stuffed olives.

2. Spear the cubes and olives on toothpicks and arrange on a platter, or go glamorous and spear them onto a whole, fresh pineapple with a pretty top. Decorate your platter with flowers. Serve to delighted guests.

IN 1965, we moved to the central mountains of Puerto Rico for Ron to begin his career as the first surgeon for the mission hospital there. We were warmly welcomed into the Aibonito community. Our new friends delighted in introducing us to the local cuisine and gladly shared their recipes for the savory rice and bean dishes and the mouth-watering chicken (*pollo*) and pork (*lechon, pernil*).

Some of the specialties which we love, such as the *pasteles*, a kind of Puerto Rican version of tamales, require an expert Puerto Rican cook, so we've never made them ourselves, relying on those experts to supply us for special occasions. Among the desserts we declare "out-of-this-world delicious" is Valetta's Coco Flan, which is a coconut custard.

Pork Chops (*Chuletas*) a la Mrs. Comas

Serves 8 • *Prep. Time: 15 minutes* • *Marinating Time: 12 hours* • *Cooking/Baking Time: 1½ hours*

8-10 ½"-thick pork chops, trimmed of excess fat, rinsed and patted dry

salt

freshly ground black pepper

1 tsp. ground cumin

1 Tbsp. dried oregano

4-6 garlic cloves, finely minced

2 Tbsp. flour

2 Tbsp. olive oil

1 cup water

4 Tbsp. soy sauce

1. Line up the chops on your cutting board. Sprinkle sparingly with salt on both sides and generously with pepper.

2. Divide the cumin, oregano, and garlic among the chops, pressing the seasonings into both sides of the meat.

3. Allow the chops to marinate overnight and absorb the flavors in the refrigerator, but cover tightly to keep the aromas where they belong.

4. Before cooking, dust the chops lightly with the flour.

5. Heat the oil in a large, heavy skillet.

6. Brown the chops briefly, a few at a time, just long enough to give the edges a pretty, caramelized color. Transfer them to a large, shallow baking pan and place them in a single layer.

7. Pour off any excess fat from the skillet. Then add a cup of water and soy sauce to the skillet, scraping up any brown bits left in the pan. Pour this over the chops.

8. Cover tightly with foil. Bake for one hour at 325°, or until the chops are tender and only a small amount of liquid remains. If the pan gets dry before the chops are done, add a little more water.

Mrs. Comas *was one of our favorite Puerto Rican cooks. We were privileged to be invited to her home for dinner.*

Before she served our meal, she fed the birds, and what a sight that was! Whole flocks of little banana quits were waiting outside in her patio for their supper. They had obviously let all their friends know about the free repast. What a chirping and singing!

After the great meal she served us, we felt like singing, too.

White Rice a la Caribe

Serves 6 • *Prep. Time: 5 minutes* • *Cooking Time: 30-40 minutes*

2 cups medium, or
short-grain, rice

3 cups water

1 tsp. salt

3 Tbsp. vegetable oil

1. Wash the rice several times, draining well.

2. Combine the rice, water, salt, and oil in a rice kettle, or a heavy kettle with a tight-fitting lid. Stir once to mix.

3. Bring to a boil, uncovered. As soon as it boils, reduce the heat to medium-low, cooking until water no longer shows above the rice.

4. Lift the rice gently from bottom to top with a wooden spoon or spatula.

5. Cover the kettle tightly and set the heat very low. Cook about 30 minutes.

6. Uncover. Again lift and turn the rice from bottom to top. Test for doneness. If it's very dry or not tender, you can add a tablespoon or two of water and steam further.

ALTHOUGH I KNOW *how Puerto Rican plain rice is done, I never seem to get quite the same perfect results as the local cooks. Theirs is even better when it's cooked in an outdoor kitchen (fogón) over a smoky fire. This recipe will get you close, but that smoky aroma and taste is impossible to duplicate.*

Sofrito

Makes about 3 cups • *Prep. Time: 5 minutes* • *Cooking Time: 10 minutes*

½ cup olive oil

3 medium onions, chopped

5-8 large garlic cloves, minced

1 large green bell pepper, chopped, or a
combination of red and green

3 slices smoked bacon, minced

1 tsp. dried oregano

1½ - 2 cups smoked ham in small cubes

½ cup cilantro, chopped, or 4-5 culantro
(*recao*) leaves, minced

2 packets of Sazon with culantro

1. Sauté onions, garlic, green
   pepper, and minced bacon in
   the oil until soft.

2. Add oregano, ham, cilantro,
   and Sazon.

3. Stir well. Set aside for the
   Beans in Sauce (opposite).

COOK'S NOTE

*Culantro and
cilantro are
similar in flavor,
but differ in
shape, size, and
intensity.
The culantro
plant has a
long, flat leaf. In
Puerto Rico it is
"recao."
Cilantro is
milder in flavor,
with the look of
flat-leaf parsley.
Coriander is the
seed of cilantro
and is different
in flavor from
the fresh leaf.*

COOK'S NOTE

*Sazon means "seasoning" in Spanish.
The packets are available in Latin
or Asian markets. To make your
own Sazon, mix 1 Tablespoon each
of salt, ground black pepper, garlic
powder, ground coriander, ground
cumin, oregano, and ground achiote
seed. The achiote (annatto) is what
makes the Sazon orange. You could
substitute paprika for the achiote.
One packet of Sazon equals 1½
teaspoons of seasoning mix. Store
extras in an airtight container.*

BEFORE YOU PREPARE *the Beans in Sauce, you'll need a
sofrito. Sofrito is the backbone for many Puerto Rican dishes,
although the recipe varies slightly from kitchen to kitchen.
It's found commercially in many supermarkets, but we've
always made our own.*

*This freezes well, so save time on your next Puerto Rican
feast and make extra.*

Beans in Sauce
Habichuelas Guisadas

Serves 8-10 • *Prep. Time: 10 minutes* • *Cooking Time: 30-40 minutes*

2 cups calabaza (squash), peeled, and cut in 1" cubes.

1 packet Sazon, or more to taste (see Cook's Note, page 164)

2 cubes chicken bouillon

2 cups water

1½ cups sofrito (see page 164)

3 15-oz. cans pink beans with liquid

½ cup fresh cilantro, coarsely chopped, or 4 whole leaves of culantro (*recao*) (see Cook's Note page 164)

1. In a large kettle, combine calabaza (squash), Sazon, bouillon cubes, and water. Bring to a boil. Cook until the squash is just tender.

2. Add the prepared sofrito and the beans with their liquid. Bring to a boil again. Reduce heat and simmer uncovered for 5-10 minutes.

3. Add cilantro.

4. Adjust seasonings by adding more salt or Sazon.

5. To slightly thicken the sauce, mash some of the squash and some of the beans against the side of the pan. Serve with White Rice a la Caribe (page 163).

TRADITION-LOVING *Puerto Rican cooks will start with dried beans, an overnight operation with admittedly excellent results. Our recipe is a shortcut method, using canned beans, but rich and delicious, nonetheless, and a great favorite with our family.*

Calabaza is a West Indian pumpkin, dense and creamy. When I can't find it, I substitute butternut squash.

Plantain Fritters

Tostones

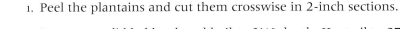

Prep. Time: 10 minutes • Cooking Time: 20-30 minutes

one large green
plantain for every
two or three
people

oil for deep frying

salt

1. Peel the plantains and cut them crosswise in 2-inch sections.

2. In a roomy, lidded kettle, add oil to 2½" depth. Heat oil to 275°-300°.

3. Put the plantain sections in the oil, avoiding crowding. You may have to do this in several batches.

4. Cover the kettle and cook 5-10 minutes or more. You don't want them to brown during this phase, but they need to test tender. Lift one out with a large, slotted spoon and press it to see if it gives to the touch.

5. When the plantains test tender, lift them out of the oil one by one. Set them upright on one side of a very damp towel, and lay the other side of the towel over them.

6. Using a small, heavy saucepan with a flat bottom, press against the plantain pieces, mashing them until they are quite flat.

7. Repeat frying and mashing with all the plantain pieces.

8. Increase the oil temperature to 350°-370°, or until very hot but not smoking.

9. Slip the tostones one at a time down the side of the kettle into the hot oil. Do not crowd. Fry a few minutes, watching closely, until crispy brown.

10. Remove with tongs and drain on paper towels. Season generously with salt and serve immediately, while still hot and crisp.

COOK'S NOTE
To make ahead, freeze the plantains after mashing. Don't thaw them. Just proceed with step 8.

THESE PLANTAIN FRITTERS *made a restaurant in Salinas, Puerto Rico, famous. Their recipe was a well-kept secret for years, until the cooks revealed their method in a TV cooking demonstration. They had two pots of oil, and two people to keep the process going.*

We've simplified the process, reducing it to one pot and one cook. Plus you can do the first step days or weeks ahead of time.

You won't complain about the results from our version. They may not be quite as air-filled as the restaurant version, but the soft centers and crispy exteriors are delicious and satisfying. Always serve them immediately. They do not reheat well.

Fried Sweet Plantains
Maduros

Prep. Time: 10 minutes • Cooking Time: 10-20 minutes

As an easy, but delicious alternative to the tostones, try the ripe plantain version. Start with ripe plantains which are yellow with black spots. Peel, then slice each plantain lengthwise in 3 or 4 slices. Sauté in equal amounts of butter and canola oil until browned on both sides. Serve hot or warm.

Readying the cooked tostone for mashing.

Mashed tostone ready for frying.

Fried tostones, salted and ready to serve.

Caribbean Salad
Ensalada Mixta

1. Line a platter with garden lettuce leaves, and arrange slices of tomato, avocados, onion, artichokes, and green pepper strips over the top. Add hearts of palm, if you wish.

2. Serve with a simple vinaigrette dressing (see pages 73, 100, and 113), or go native and have cruets of vinegar and olive oil, plus salt and pepper, for guests to dress their own salads to taste.

Valetta's Coco Flan

Serves 10-12   •   Prep. Time: 5 minutes   •   Cooking/Baking Time: 2 hours   •   Chilling Time: 3-4 hours

1 cup granulated sugar

15-oz. can cream of coconut (we like Coco Lopez)

14-oz. can sweetened condensed milk; low-fat is fine

12-oz. can evaporated milk; low-fat is fine

5 eggs

dash salt

OUR FRIEND, VALETTA BONILLA, *is famous in Aibonito for her perfect coconut flan. Fortunately for us, she did not keep her recipe a family secret.*

Don't count the calories in this recipe, but make the servings small. This is very rich and out-of-this-world delicious. We usually make the flan a day or two ahead of the party.

1. In a heavy skillet, cook the sugar, stirring it continuously over low heat just until golden.

2. Pour the caramelized sugar into a 9"×13" baking pan and coat the bottom and the sides of the pan. Set it aside to cool and harden. Important: if you are using a glass or ceramic pan, allow it to heat in the preheating oven before pouring in the caramelized sugar to avoid the risk of cracking the pan. Then set it aside to harden before adding the colder custard mixture.

3. Combine the remaining ingredients and beat very well in a blender. Beat for several minutes, says Valetta.

4. Pour mixture into the prepared flan pan.

5. Set the pan in a larger pan, and pour cold water around the outside of the flan pan.

6. Set it in the oven and bake at 350° just until the water in the outside pan is hot, about 10 minutes.

7. Now lower the oven temperature to 250° and continue baking for 1 hour. Check if the custard is set. If it is not, continue baking and checking every 20 minutes, up to 2 hours, until the custard is just set.

8. Cool completely. Chill in the refrigerator for several hours before serving.

9. Serve it directly from the baking pan, or invert it onto a rimmed plate to catch that rich, caramel syrup. Cut into squares to serve.

169

An Indian Feast

Steamed Basmati Rice

Ellie's Gorgeous Dhal

Minnie's Classic Chicken and Potato Curry

Spinach and Paneer

Fresh Tomato Chutney

Cucumber and Yogurt Raita

The Indian Breads:
Puris, Naan, and Pappadums

Major Grey's Mango Chutney (purchased)

Rippled Ice-Cream Sherbet Pie

MORE THAN 50 YEARS after he left India at the age of 13 with his parents and younger sister, my husband Ron returned to his birthplace. It seemed that little had changed – the heat and dust, the wandering cattle, the exotic colors and heady aromas. Everything brought back memories of his childhood.

But the food memories were the deepest. Ah, those wonderful curries and their equally wonderful accompaniments! He reveled in the rich and varied flavors (and kept the antacids handy).

Fortunately, we can duplicate many of those dishes far from India. Most of the spices we need can be found in our local Asian market, or we can send for them online. If you have a craving for such things as lime pickle (hot!) or spicy eggplant relish (also hot!), add those to your market basket for the condiment tray, along with the toasted coconut, roasted peanuts, raisins, and Major Grey's Mango Chutney.

Ron's mother, also known as Grandma Minnie, learned the tricks of Indian cuisine from the local cooks of the Central Provinces. She prepared everything from the Indian breads and fritters to several kinds of sweets, in addition to the curry and rice dishes.

What we've included here are some of our favorite Indian dishes, including breads, chutneys, and some vegetarian treats, in addition to the curry. For a family reunion of 30 people, we put together a wide variety of these dishes.

Steamed Basmati Rice

Serves 6-8 • *Prep. Time: 5 minutes* • *Cooking Time: 25-35 minutes*

COOK'S NOTE

For Jasmine Rice, simply substitute jasmine rice for the basmati rice, use the same additional ingredients, and follow these same instructions.

2½ cups uncooked basmati rice

5 cups water

1 tsp. salt

1 Tbsp. butter

1. Combine the rice, water, salt, and butter in a 4-quart saucepan.

2. Place the saucepan over high heat and, when the water begins to boil, reduce the heat to low and stir the rice once.

3. Cover tightly and continue to cook on low heat until all the liquid is absorbed, 15-20 minutes. Fluff with a fork before serving.

COOK'S NOTE

This recipe makes great rice without a rice cooker (but use a rice cooker if you have it).

The grandchildren engrossed in a game while the Mamas cook.

Ellie's Gorgeous Dhal

Serves 8 • Prep. Time: 20 minutes
Cooking Time: 35-45 minutes, plus reheating 20 minutes • Cooling Time: 2 hours

1½ cups orange lentils

1 tsp. turmeric

3 whole, thin, green, serrano chiles

4-4½ cups water

1-1½ tsp. salt, to taste

4 Tbsp. oil

1 medium onion, chopped

2 cloves garlic, minced

1 Tbsp. grated ginger root

4 small bay leaves

4 tiny, dried red chili peppers

¾ cup canned, diced tomatoes

1 tsp. salt, or to taste

cilantro, to garnish

1. In a large saucepan cook the lentils, turmeric and green chilies over medium heat, in water to cover. As they cook, add a little oil to reduce foaming. Remove foam if necessary.

2. Cook for 8-10 minutes. The lentils should be just al dente at this point.

3. In a skillet, fry the onion, garlic, and ginger in the oil until the onion is translucent.

4. Add the bay leaves and dried red chilies to the skillet, stirring them around so they heat through and to release their flavor.

5. Add the tomatoes to the onion mixture, stirring until heated through.

6. Now add the tomato mixture to the cooked lentils.

7. Continue to cook this gently, stirring occasionally until it is the consistency you want and the lentils are totally soft. If it is too thick, add water. If it is too thin, keep cooking it down. Add one teaspoon of salt, then taste and adjust salt.

8. Allow to cool. Refrigerate until shortly before your Indian dinner. Heat gently, stirring occasionally to prevent sticking, until heated through.

9. Before serving remove the green chilies, bay leaves, and red chiles (they may have turned black).

10. Garnish with sprigs of cilantro.

RON'S SISTER, *Eleanor Kreider, who was also born in India, is another superb cook with a special touch for Indian cuisine. This is one of her delicious vegetarian dishes.*

Make this dhal one or two days before you serve your Indian dinner for the best flavor, although it's fine to eat it right away. The different elements begin to marry after the first day. It just gets better.

PLAN TO MAKE *this curry the day before or early in the morning on the day you plan to serve it. The flavors need time to develop. If you're serving it the same day, don't refrigerate. Just cover and hold. For next-day service, refrigerate overnight. Gently reheat to serve.*

Minnie's Classic Chicken and Potato Curry

Serves 8 • *Prep. Time: 20 minutes* • *Cooking Time: 50-60 minutes*

4 Tbsp. your favorite curry powder

⅓ cup vegetable oil

1 large onion, chopped

4 large cloves garlic, minced

1 Tbsp. freshly grated ginger root

3 lbs. boneless, skinless chicken thighs, cut into 1" chunks, trimmed of excess fat

15-oz. can chopped tomatoes

½ cup chopped, fresh cilantro, or 4-5 leaves culantro (*dhania*)

1 tsp. salt

2-4 cups water

2 medium potatoes, diced

2 tsp. garam masala

¼ cup chopped cilantro, for garnish

1. Mix and heat the curry powder in a small dry skillet, stirring and roasting till aromatic, 1-2 minutes. Take care not to burn. Set aside.

2. In a large skillet or kettle, heat the vegetable oil.

3. Add onion, garlic, and ginger root. Cook over low heat for 4 minutes.

4. Add all the curry powder, stirring well.

5. Add the chicken chunks. Stir to coat well with the curry/onion mixture, about 3 minutes.

6. Add chopped tomatoes, chopped cilantro or culantro (*dhania*), salt, and water to cover. Simmer 20 minutes.

7. Add diced potatoes. Cover and cook till potatoes are tender, 15-25 minutes. Taste for salt and adjust as needed. Do not overcook.

8. To finish, sprinkle with garam masala and ¼ cup chopped cilantro. Let cool, uncovered. Then cover and hold till time to serve. If making a day ahead, refrigerate. Heat to serve, but do not boil.

COOK'S NOTE
In Puerto Rico culantro is recao and in India it is called "dhania" (see Cook's note on page 164 for an explanation of the difference between cilantro and culantro). Grandma would chop up her dhania, form it into small balls, and freeze for her wintertime curries.

Spinach and Paneer

Serves 6 • *Prep. Time: 15 minutes* • *Cooking Time: 20-30 minutes*

2-3 Tbsp. vegetable oil

1 medium onion, chopped

4 cloves garlic, crushed

1" cube ginger root, minced

2 tsp. ground coriander

2 tsp. garam masala

1 tsp. ground cumin

1 tsp. chili powder

½ tsp. turmeric

salt, to taste

15-oz. can crushed tomatoes

10-oz pkg. frozen chopped spinach, thawed

7-10 oz. paneer, cut into small cubes

1 green chili pepper, minced, *optional*

1. Sauté the onion, garlic and ginger in the oil until lightly browned.

2. Stir in all the spices and cook, stirring, for a minute or two, to refresh the spice.

3. Add the tomatoes. Cook until the oil appears on the surface, about 3 minutes.

4. Add spinach and paneer.

5. Cover the pan and cook on low for 7 minutes. Add a bit of water if mixture seems dry. Taste before adding the green chili pepper!

THIS LOVELY DISH, *a North Indian specialty, features cooked spinach with a delicate Indian cheese called paneer. You can buy paneer at any Asian market, or make your own by following the easy recipe included with the Ricotta recipe on page 232.*

The red chili powder gives the whole dish a nice subtle heat, but if you want a more intense bite, stir in the fresh green chili pepper at the end.

Fresh Tomato Chutney

Makes 3½ cups • *Prep. Time: 20 minutes*

⅓ cup water

2 Tbsp. cider vinegar

1 Tbsp. sugar

⅛ tsp. salt, or to taste

freshly ground black pepper, to taste

2 cups diced fresh tomatoes

½ cup chopped green bell pepper

½ cup cucumber, diced

½ cup finely chopped sweet onion

snipped cilantro, as much as you like

1. Mix the water, vinegar, sugar, salt, and black pepper in a bowl.

2. Add the tomatoes, green pepper, cucumber, onion, and cilantro. Mix it all up.

3. Chill until ready to serve.

COOK'S NOTE
We prefer Vidalia onions for this recipe, but a Spanish onion will serve.

Cucumber and Yogurt Raita

Makes about 3 cups • *Prep. Time: 10 minutes* • *Cooking Time: 2-5 minutes*

⅛ tsp. cumin seeds

⅛ tsp. mustard seeds

2 cups plain yogurt

1 small cucumber, peeled and grated

1 Tbsp. minced cilantro, or more to taste

1 Tbsp. chopped fresh mint, chopped

salt, to taste

1. Toast the cumin and mustard seeds in a small dry skillet, shaking or stirring, until they become aromatic and mustard seeds begin to pop, 2-5 minutes. Set aside to cool.

2. Just stir it all together, top with the toasted seeds, and serve it in a pretty bowl.

IF YOUR DINNER *features a hot and spicy curry, everyone will be grateful if you serve plain yogurt. But this cooling combination of yogurt and cucumber makes an especially lovely addition to the Indian meal. Some cooks add a minced green chili if they want extra heat.*

Emma, Sibyl's daughter, with one of the family chickens (definitely not destined for curry!)

The Indian Breads:
Puris, Naan, and Pappadums

CHAPTER 9
CELEBRATIONS
AN INDIAN
FEAST

PURIS

Prep. Time: 15-20 minutes • Cooking Time: 2-5 minutes per puri

⅔ cup whole wheat flour

⅔ cup all-purpose flour

¼ tsp. salt

¼ tsp. cardamom powder, *optional*

2 Tbsp. oil

½ cup lukewarm water

oil for deep-frying

1. Combine flours, salt, optional cardamom, 2 Tbsp. oil, and water in a small bowl.

2. On a floured board, knead until smooth and elastic, 3-5 minutes.

3. Divide dough into 16 pieces. Roll each into a thin, 3"-4" circle.

4. Pour oil in kettle to depth of 2"-2½". Heat oil to 350°.

5. Fry one puri at a time, pushing it down into the oil until it puffs, then turning it over to fry the other side for a minute or two, until lightly browned.

6. Remove and drain on paper towels.

NAAN
(see page 59)

PAPPADUMS

Prep. Time: 5 minutes • Cooking Time: 30 seconds per Pappadum

1. You will need to purchase these at an Asian market. Usually, in addition to the plain pappadums, you will have a choice of seasoned, some of which will be quite spicy.

2. Cut them in half or in quarters and drop into hot oil (325°-350°) using tongs. The pappadum will practically explode, expanding and crisping up beautifully. It happens fast!

3. Remove from the oil and drain on paper towels. Plan to make them shortly before you serve the meal so they retain their crispness. Serve in a large basket lined with paper napkins or a paper towel.

WE LIKE *to have an Indian bread to accompany an Indian meal. If you don't have time to make the Naan or the Puris, consider serving Pappadums. They're quick and easy.*

THIS ISN'T AN INDIAN DESSERT, *but it's a cool and delicious ending to a spicy meal. You'll find that it's easy to prepare, and everyone simply loves it.*

The orange zest in the chocolate sauce is that extra touch that lifts this pie out of the ordinary.

Rippled Ice Cream Sherbet Pie

Prep. Time: 20 minutes • Baking/Cooking Time: 20 minutes • Chilling Time: 6 hours or overnight

1⅓ cups vanilla wafer crumbs

⅓ cup unsweetened cocoa powder

⅓ cup powdered sugar

5⅓ Tbsp. (⅓ cup) butter, melted

6 oz. chocolate chips

¾ cup evaporated milk

½ tsp. grated orange rind

1 pint vanilla ice cream

1 pint orange sherbet

1. Combine vanilla wafer crumbs, cocoa powder, powdered sugar, and melted butter in a small bowl.

2. Press into bottom and up sides of a 9" pie plate to form a crust. Bake for 10 minutes at 325°.

3. Remove from oven and cool completely. Chill. (If time is short, you could substitute a purchased chocolate crumb crust.)

4. In a small saucepan, combine the chocolate chips, evaporated milk, and grated orange rind. Cook and stir constantly over low heat till melted and smooth. Cool.

5. Assemble the pie as follows: pour ⅓ of the chocolate/orange sauce into the bottom of the cookie-crumb crust.

6. Arrange alternate scoops of vanilla ice cream and orange sherbet over the layer of sauce. Top with ⅓ of the sauce.

7. Arrange another layer of scoops of vanilla ice cream and orange sherbet over this layer, making sure your vanilla scoops are atop the orange scoops of the bottom layer and the orange atop the vanilla. Top with the final ⅓ of the sauce.

8. Return to the freezer and freeze firm, 6 hours or overnight.

9. Cut in wedges to serve, and for an extra touch, drizzle a little warm chocolate sauce over each serving. (See recipe, page 102.)

COOK'S NOTE
You could make this with lime sherbet and grated lime rind instead of the orange.

CHAPTER 10

The Thai Dinner

Thai Ginger Chicken Soup

Chicken or Beef Satay

Peanut Sauce & Cucumber Sauce

Thai Sweet and Sour Vegetables

Jasmine Rice (see page 172)

Thai Ginger Chicken Soup

Serves 6-8 as first course, 4 as a main course • *Prep. Time: 25 minutes* • *Cooking Time: 10 minutes*

3 cups light coconut milk

2 cups water, or chicken broth

½ lb. boneless chicken breast (about half of a large breast) cut in strips

1" section of ginger root, peeled and thinly sliced

1 Tbsp. fish sauce, or more, to taste

¼ cup fresh lime juice

2 Kaffir lime leaves

1 tsp. chili paste (*sambal oeleck*), *or* to taste

2-3 tsp. brown sugar, to taste

FOR GARNISH:

2 Tbsp. sliced green onions

1 Tbsp. chopped cilantro

1-3 red chili peppers, seeded and slivered

sprigs of cilantro

OPTIONAL ADDITIONS:
(to make this a main course)

straw mushrooms

miniature corn

bamboo shoots

1. Bring coconut milk and water to a boil. Reduce heat to medium-low.

2. Add chicken and cook for 3 minutes.

3. Stir in ginger, fish sauce, lime juice, Kaffir lime leaves, chili paste, and brown sugar. This is the time to taste and adjust the seasoning.

4. To serve, sprinkle with green onions and cilantro.

5. Garnish with the red pepper slivers and the sprigs of cilantro.

6. Top with Optional Additions if you want to make this a main course.

COOK'S NOTE
Kaffir lime leaves – wonderful, if you can get them. Otherwise, substitute ¼ tsp. lime zest.

COOK'S NOTE
Do you happen to own a Mongolian hot pot? It's a great way to serve this soup. Otherwise, just ladle it from your cooking kettle into small individual bowls and place at each table setting.

THE RECIPE is surprisingly simple to prepare. You can make it first and hold it back to reheat at the last minute, while you grill the satay and stir-fry the vegetables. Just wait to add the final touches of green onion and cilantro; otherwise, they will darken.

Also, remember that the ginger slices will keep adding heat and flavor to the soup, so you may want to remove some of them if the soup is going to wait awhile before serving.

If you want to turn this into a main course, serve it with steamed rice, and round out the soup with the Optional Additions at the end of the recipe.

Chicken or Beef Satay

Serves 4 • *Prep. Time: 20 minutes* • *Marinating Time: 2 hours* • *Grilling Time: 5-20 minutes*

1 lb. boneless chicken breast, beef, or pork, or a combination of the three

3 Tbsp. oil

1 stalk fresh lemongrass, or the zest from ½ lemon

3 cloves garlic

½ tsp. red chili peppers, seeded, *optional*

1 Tbsp. curry powder

1 tsp. sugar, or honey

1 tsp. fish sauce, or ¼ tsp. salt

1. Cut chicken, beef, or pork into 2" strips.

2. In a food processor or blender combine oil, lemon grass, garlic, red chili peppers if you wish, curry powder, sugar or honey and fish sauce. Blend until smooth.

3. Pour over meat. Marinate for two hours.

4. Thread meat onto skewers. Grill or broil, turning occasionally, until cooked.

5. Serve with Peanut Sauce (page 186) and Cucumber Sauce (page 187) on the side.

COOK'S NOTE

Lemongrass: To use fresh lemongrass, cut away the top green part of the stalk and the root tip. You'll use the bulb section in the marinade, but don't throw away the leaves as they make a wonderful tea. Lemongrass can also be chopped and stored in the freezer. If you don't have lemongrass, the zest of a lemon is the best substitute.

COOK'S NOTE

If you are using bamboo or wooden skewers, be sure to soak them in water for 10-20 minutes before threading on the meat.

COOK'S NOTE

The quality of your satay will depend on the quality of the beef and pork. Choose a beef or pork cut that will not need tenderizing. If you want to substitute shrimp for the chicken/beef/pork, simply reduce the marinating time to 20-30 minutes.

Peanut Sauce

Makes about 2 cups • *Prep. Time: 10 minutes*

2 tsp. chopped ginger root

2 cloves garlic, chopped

¼ cup red wine vinegar

¼ cup soy sauce

1 cup creamy peanut butter

½ to 1 serrano pepper, or more, depending on how hot you like it. Or substitute hot chili sauce or hot oil, to taste.

⅓ cup honey

2 tsp. dark sesame oil

2 tsp. curry powder

1 Tbsp. fresh cilantro, or more, to taste

COOK'S NOTE

Dry-toast the curry powder to enhance the flavor. In a small skillet stir the curry powder constantly over medium heat until lightly browned and aromatic. It happens fast, so don't let it burn!

1. Process the ginger root, garlic, red wine vinegar, soy sauce and peanut butter in your food processor until well blended.

2. Add the serrano or pepper sauce, the honey, sesame oil, and curry powder. Blend until smooth. Taste and adjust seasonings.

3. Add the fresh cilantro and process only briefly, so you can still see the bits of green.

4. Scrape the sauce out into a pretty ceramic serving bowl. Serve at room temperature. Or if you want to warm it, use a low setting on your microwave just before serving. Be careful not to boil it.

WE ORIGINALLY FOLLOWED *a recipe in a Thai cookbook for a satay peanut sauce that was delicious, but complicated and time-consuming to prepare. Then we found this simpler and equally delicious alternative, which is much easier to make! No cooking. Everything goes in the food processor. What could be better?*

Cucumber Sauce

Makes about 2 cups • *Prep. Time: 10 minutes*

2 Tbsp. sugar

1 tsp. salt

3 Tbsp. white vinegar

5 Tbsp. water

1 English cucumber, thinly sliced

fresh cilantro, chopped, to taste

1 small carrot, finely grated, *optional*

1 shallot, thinly sliced, *optional*

1. In a medium-sized bowl, combine the sugar, salt, vinegar, and water, stirring until the sugar dissolves.

2. Add the cucumbers with the freshly snipped cilantro, the optional carrot, and shallot. Stir gently to combine.

REFRESHING, CRUNCHY *and super easy to throw together, this is a key side dish for the satay meal, or any Thai grilled food.*

Thai Sweet and Sour Vegetables

Serves 6-8 • *Prep. Time: 20 minutes* • *Cooking Time: 3-5 minutes*

Mixed vegetables (allow 1½-2 cups
sliced vegetables per person)

SELECT FROM THE FOLLOWING:
Fresh: (choose three or four)

bell peppers •

string beans •

asparagus •

zucchini •

mushrooms •

tomatoes •

onions •

Canned: *(choose one or two or all three)*

water chestnuts •

bamboo shoots •

miniature corn •

¼ cup tomato sauce, or ketchup

2 Tbsp. red wine vinegar

1-2 Tbsp. fish sauce

2 Tbsp. sugar

½ tsp. salt

4-6 red chili peppers, sliced, *optional*

2 Tbsp. oil

3 cloves garlic, finely chopped

2 Tbsp. cornstarch

½ cup water

chopped cilantro, for garnish

1. Cut fresh vegetables into 1"- 2" strips.

2. Combine the tomato sauce or ketchup, red wine vinegar, fish sauce, sugar, salt, and the red chili peppers, if desired. Adjust seasoning to taste. Set aside.

3. Heat oil and garlic in a large skillet or wok on medium heat until garlic is golden brown.

4. Add all the vegetables and stir-fry 1-2 minutes.

5. Stir the tomato sauce mixture into the vegetable mixture in your wok.

6. Combine the cornstarch and water, blending to make a smooth paste. Add the cornstarch mixture to the wok. Cook 5 minutes, or until vegetables are cooked and sauce is thickened. Garnish with cilantro.

7. Serve immediately with jasmine rice. Follow the directions for Steamed Basmati Rice (see page 172), substituting jasmine rice for the basmati.

CHAPTER 11

A Taste of Bulgaria

Roasted Eggplant and Garlic Salad
Kyopoulo

Snow White Salad
Snejanka

Tomato, Cucumber, and Cheese Salad
Shopska Salata

Round Loaf
Pitka

Grilled Pork Skewers
Shishcheta

Roasted Herbed New Potatoes
Pecheni Kartofi

Dani's Honey Walnut Baklava

DAUGHTER SUSAN says the typical Bulgarian meal must absolutely start with a salad course – in order to have something to accompany the *rakia*, that all-important glass of grape or plum sipping brandy, served icy cold at the start of a meal. The salad of choice would be the indispensable *shopska salata*, Bulgaria's national dish, consisting of chopped cucumber, tomato, and fresh white Bulgarian feta cheese.

Bulgarians are famous for stretching dinner out for hours. The starters and salads trickle out to the table, a little more bread is served, another round of *rakia* is poured into tiny glasses, the conversation gets animated, and almost without notice the main courses begin to arrive, invariably no longer hot, but at room temperature – and nobody seems to mind.

Lightly seasoned grilled meats are most common, served with potatoes, usually fried or sautéed in butter. To finish off a meal, a platter of sliced fresh fruit is usually served, whatever is in season – apricots, apples, strawberries, or watermelon. This is an incredibly satisfying end to a heavy meal. In the fall and winter, baklava is a common dessert, a slice of history held over from Ottoman occupation.

The menu Susan has chosen is a compilation of some of her favorite Bulgarian starters and sides, with a twist on the traditional timing. Instead of having separate courses, she puts everything out on the table just before the final call of the grill-master: "Meat's ready!" Then the roasted potatoes come straight out of the oven, the meat is piping

Grandkids Maddie (left) and Evelyn enjoy a bit of Bulgarian culture.

hot off the grill, and everything is served as one big colorful feast.

The seasoning of the meat is done with a light touch, making it the perfect complement to the intensely flavorful dips, spreads, and salads, giving your guests the pleasure of discovering unique and varied combinations. Take your time…*Nazdrave*! To your health!

Roasted Eggplant and Garlic Salad (*Kyopoulo*)

4 cups • *Prep. Time: 20 minutes* • *Baking Time: 20-40 minutes*

3 medium eggplants

4 red sweet peppers (Bulgarian heirloom…if you can get them!)

2 medium tomatoes

1 head garlic with cloves intact

2 Tbsp. olive oil, *divided*

½ cup parsley, coarsely chopped

1 Tbsp. red wine vinegar

1 tsp. salt

½ tsp. freshly ground black pepper

fresh parsley sprig

1. Place the eggplants, peppers, tomatoes, and head of garlic in a shallow, foil-lined roasting pan.

2. Drizzle with 1 Tbsp. oil and toss the pan gently to coat the veggies.

3. Place in the upper rack of your oven near the heat source. Broil. As the veggies brown, turn them with tongs until most of the sides are charred. This could take 20-30 minutes.

4. Remove the pan from the oven. Pinch together the edges of the foil in the pan, enclosing the vegetables so they can steam for about 10 minutes.

5. Open the foil package. Remove charred peel from vegetables, leaving a few little charred flecks for flavor and visual effect.

6. Put the vegetables in a sieve to drain, pressing down lightly to squeeze out excess liquid. This step will keep the kyopoulo thick and prevent watery edges from forming while it waits to be served.

7. Put the veggies, parsley, vinegar, remaining 1 Tbsp. oil, salt and pepper into a food processor and pulse 5-8 times for a chunky consistency.

8. Pour into a serving bowl and garnish with a sprig of parsley. Serve at room temperature.

Snow White Salad
(*Snejanka*)

1½ cups • *Prep. Time: 15 minutes* • *Chilling Time: 1-12 hours*

2 cups plain yogurt

1 garlic clove

½ tsp. salt

2 tsp. olive oil

2 cucumbers, crisp English or
Asian variety

1 Tbsp. fresh dill

¼ cup walnuts, finely chopped

1. Put the yogurt in a cheesecloth-lined mesh sieve and set the sieve over a bowl. Refrigerate. Drain for at least 1 hour, or overnight for much thicker yogurt.

2. Chop the garlic and mash to a smooth paste, using the salt and the back of a wooden spoon.

3. In a small bowl, whisk together the yogurt, garlic paste, and olive oil.

4. Peel, seed, and finely dice the cucumbers. Then squeeze the diced cucumber gently in a clean kitchen towel to remove excess water.

5. Finely chop the dill.

6. Stir the cucumber, dill, and chopped walnuts into the yogurt mixture. Serve chilled.

THIS SALAD *can be thick enough to scoop into ball-shaped servings, or presented in a bowl as a sauce. It all depends on how much liquid you drain out of your yogurt. Drain it overnight in the refrigerator for a seriously rich spread, or only one hour to achieve the consistency pictured on page 192. Either way, you'll need to start this salad in advance.*

Tomato, Cucumber, and Cheese Salad (*Shopska Salata*)

Serves 6 • *Prep. Time: 15 minutes*

4 medium tomatoes, chopped

3 small cucumbers, seeded and chopped

4 green onions, chopped

2 small green Bulgarian Heirloom peppers, seeded and chopped

salt and pepper, to taste

red wine vinegar, to taste

olive oil, to taste

1 cup Bulgarian feta, grated

¼ cup chopped parsley

1. Place tomatoes, cucumbers, onions, and peppers in a bowl. Lightly salt and pepper.

2. Add a very small dash of red wine vinegar and a quick drizzle of olive oil. Toss very gently.

3. Mound the grated cheese on top and garnish with the parsley.

4. Toss gently again at the table, right before serving. Add more salt and pepper individually, to taste.

IF EVER THERE WAS *a national dish, this would have to be it. No Bulgarian meal is complete without this fresh, flavorful salad. Bulgarian feta is more creamy and less salty than Greek.*

Bulgarian Heirloom peppers are difficult to come by. If you need to, substitute with Hungarian peppers, which are readily available.

BREAD TRADITIONS ABOUND *in Bulgaria. Bread is* *essential to every meal. This round loaf can be made a* *day in advance and warmed on the upper shelf of the grill* *wrapped in foil while the skewers cook.*

Round Loaf (*Pitka*)

Prep. Time: 30 minutes • *Rising Time: 45-60 minutes* • *Baking Time: 45-50 minutes*

3½- 4 cups all-purpose
flour, *divided*

1 Tbsp. instant dry yeast

1 tsp. salt

1 Tbsp. sugar

1¼ cups whole milk

3 Tbsp. butter

1 egg, separated

1. In a bowl, whisk together 3½ cups flour, yeast, salt, and sugar.

2. In a small saucepan mix together the milk, butter, and egg yolk. Warm on the stove over medium heat until the butter begins to melt.

3. Remove from the heat and stir until the butter is completely melted.

4. Stir the lukewarm milk mixture into the flour mixture with a wooden spoon, or your hands, until fully incorporated.

5. Turn the dough out onto the counter and knead for a minute or two, adding more flour until the dough is no longer sticky.

6. Shape the dough into a round loaf. Place it on a greased baking sheet.

7. Cover with a clean kitchen towel. Let rise until double, 45-60 minutes.

8. Brush the top of the risen loaf gently with the reserved egg white. Bake at 400° for 45-50 minutes, until the top is deep brown.

9. Remove the baked loaf to a cooling rack. For a softer crust, cover with a clean kitchen towel until cooled. Serve on a cutting board and slice as needed.

Grilled Pork Skewers
(Shishcheta)

Serves 6 • *Prep. Time: 20 minutes* • *Chilling Time: 2 hours* • *Grilling Time: 8-10 minutes*

1½ lbs. boneless pork loin, cut into 1" cubes

1 large sweet onion, cubed

2 green bell peppers, cubed

freshly ground sea salt

freshly ground black pepper

1 Tbsp. butter, melted

1. Thread the meat and vegetable cubes onto 6 large skewers.

2. Generously salt and pepper them and let sit, covered, in the refrigerator for 2 hours.

3. Grill over medium embers, turning and brushing with melted butter until golden edges form and pork is cooked through, about 8-10 minutes.

SEASONED WITH *a light touch, these grilled pork morsels are perfect with the intensely flavorful Bulgarian salads...so serve them together for best results!*

Roasted Herbed
New Potatoes *(Pecheni Kartofi)*

Serves 6 • Prep. Time: 10 minutes • Baking Time: 30-40 minutes

2 pounds small new potatoes,
scrubbed and dried

2 Tbsp. olive oil

freshly ground sea salt

freshly ground pepper

1 Tbsp. fresh dill, finely chopped

1. In a large baking pan, toss the potatoes with the oil and generous grindings of salt and pepper.

2. Roast at 400°, tossing occasionally, for about 30-40 minutes until crisp and browned.

3. Sprinkle on the dill and toss again, then turn out into a warmed dish. Serve immediately.

SERVE THESE *straight out of the oven for the best texture – crusty and salty on the outside, creamy on the inside!*

THE ORIGIN *may be debatable and the versions innumerable, but one thing is certain: our friend Dani makes fantastic baklava. She has the recipe perfected.*

Pay attention to the temperature of the honey syrup. If it's too warm, you'll end up with a soft, cake-like bar and you'll lose the elegant layers you've created with the phyllo. But if it's too cold, the layers will not absorb enough of the syrup and the texture will be dry.

Another little secret Dani shared: egg and flour added to the walnut mixture will help keep the nuts from crumbling out when you slice servings of this decadent dessert.

COOK'S NOTE

Fresh phyllo pastry can be found at Greek or Middle Eastern markets, but is also readily available in the freezer section of large grocery stores. It's important to thaw the pastry properly and bring it to room temperature for ease of handling. So follow the directions on the package and be aware that you'll want to start that process the night before.

The 1-lb. packages contain about 20 sheets of dough. Sizes vary from brand to brand, so you may need to trim or overlap the sheets to fit your pan. Overlapping and folding the edges of the sheets is perfectly fine, but just remember to brush melted butter between them.

Dani's Honey Walnut Baklava

Makes 30 2-inch squares • *Prep. Time: 25 minutes*
Cooking/Baking Time: 40 minutes • *Standing Time: 5 hours*

THE PASTRY AND FILLING

⅓ cup sugar

1 egg

1 Tbsp. flour

1 tsp. cinnamon

3 cups chopped walnuts

1-lb. package phyllo dough

2 sticks (1 cup) unsalted butter, melted

THE SYRUP

2 cups water

1 cup sugar

1 cup honey

1 slice lemon

1. Make the filling by mixing together the sugar, egg, flour and cinnamon with a whisk. Stir in walnuts. Set aside.

2. Brush a 10"×12" baking dish with melted butter.

3. Place one sheet of phyllo dough in the bottom of the dish and brush with melted butter.

4. Place another sheet on top and brush with melted butter. Continue this until you use half the phyllo dough.

5. Pour the walnut mixture on top.

6. Layer the remaining phyllo pastry on top of the walnut filling, brushing each sheet with melted butter. Brush top with remaining butter.

7. Cut into 2" squares, cutting all the way down to the nut mixture, but not through to the bottom phyllo layers. A kitchen shears works well for this.

8. Bake at 350° until golden, about 40 minutes. Cool completely, at least 1 hour.

9. Stir syrup ingredients together in a saucepan. Bring to boil and boil for 8 minutes, stirring constantly.

10. Remove lemon. Set syrup aside until barely warm, about 104°.

11. Pour the barely warm syrup over the cooled baklava. Allow the pastry to absorb the syrup for at least 4 hours before serving.

The Fourth of July Picnic

Oven-Barbecued Chicken

Grilled Brats and Hamburgers with Fixings
(recipes not included)

Nelson's Calico Baked Beans (see page 65)

Dijon, Bacon, and Potato Salad

Creamy Coleslaw with Pineapple and Almonds

Fresh Garden Tomato and Cucumber Platter
(recipe not included)

Magic Fudge Cake and Magic Fudge Frosting

Rippled Ice Cream Sherbet Pie (see page 181)

JANE AND SCOTT'S huge lawn is the perfect spot for our Fourth of July picnic. Newly mowed, the smooth green slopes down toward the pond, where the small beach beckons invitingly to the guests who've begun to arrive in the hot afternoon. Soon the children are splashing in the water, along with some of the adults and the dogs. Others lounge on the Adirondack chairs under the trees or lazily sway on the porch swing and hammock.

Toward evening, Scott fires up the grill. The platters of fresh tomatoes and cucumbers from Jane's garden are chilled and ready for the picnic table. Bowls of potato salad, coleslaw, casseroles of baked beans, and baked barbecued chicken are ready, plus hot dogs, brats, and hamburgers for the grill. Pitchers of lemonade are standing by. We set out bags of chips and all the add-ons for the burgers.

We offer a heartfelt prayer of gratitude for friends and family gathered for this utterly American celebration, and then everyone digs in with gusto.

With the approach of darkness, the children dance about with sparklers, making patterns of light across the lawn. Later we'll head to town, toting blankets and old quilts to spread out on the grass in the park among other families to watch the town's annual fireworks display.

THIS MOUTH-WATERINGLY TENDER *chicken in a tangy, rich sauce is a good one to know because you can put it together the night before. After about an hour and a half in the oven, the sauce will be reduced to a thick glaze.*

We often use only chicken thighs and legs for this dish, as they seem to absorb the flavors best. If you use boneless thighs, cut back on the oven time.

Oven-Barbecued Chicken

Serves 8 • *Prep. Time: 10 minutes* • *Marinating Time: 12 hours* • *Baking Time: 1½ hours*

8-oz. can tomato sauce

¼ cup vegetable oil

⅓ cup fresh lemon juice

3 Tbsp. Worcestershire sauce

1 tsp. prepared mustard

1 tsp. hot pepper sauce

3 Tbsp. brown sugar

2 tsp. salt

½ cup minced onion

1 clove garlic, minced

1 Tbsp. grated fresh ginger root

3 lbs. bone-in chicken pieces, skin removed for less fat

1. Combine all the sauce ingredients in a large glass bowl. Whisk to combine well.

2. Place the chicken pieces into the sauce and stir to coat. Cover tightly and place in the refrigerator to marinate overnight.

3. Arrange the chicken pieces in a single layer in a large, shallow baking dish.

4. Pour all the marinade over the chicken.

5. Bake at 350° for ½ hour. Turn the pieces over and bake for an additional 1 hour on the other side, or until the sauce is thick and chicken is well-browned.

6. Turn off the oven. The chicken can sit, covered, in the warmed oven for ½ hour, or until you're ready to serve.

Ann's oldest son, Niles, a college student, is an entrepreneur and co-founder of Cultural Ventures, which produces Menno Tea.

You can't go wrong with this salad. We love the hint of smoke. Carefully add just enough liquid smoke to boost the bacon flavor without overpowering the salad.

Dijon, Bacon, and Potato Salad

Serves 8 • *Prep. Time: 30 minutes* • *Cooking Time: 20 minutes*

2 lbs. small, red-skinned potatoes, well-scrubbed, quartered

3 cloves garlic, peeled and smashed

1 tsp. salt

2 Tbsp. olive oil

6 slices smoked bacon, diced

1½ cups finely diced red onion

⅓ cup red wine vinegar

½ tsp. sugar

1 cup mayonnaise

¼ cup Dijon mustard

½ tsp. liquid smoke, or more, to taste

½ tsp. salt, or to taste

1. Place the quartered potatoes in a large pot along with the garlic and 1 tsp. salt. Add water to cover completely.

2. Bring to a boil over high heat, then reduce to a simmer and cook until the potatoes are fork-tender, about 20 minutes.

3. Place the olive oil in a medium skillet. Add bacon and cook over medium-high heat until the bacon is brown and crispy.

4. Drain off about half the oil. Remove from the heat and add the diced red onions, vinegar, and sugar.

5. Stir in the mayonnaise, Dijon mustard, and liquid smoke. Mix well. Set aside.

6. When the potatoes test done, drain well. Peel, if desired. Discard the garlic.

7. Transfer the potatoes to a large mixing bowl. While they are still hot, add the bacon/onion/mayonnaise mixture. Stir to combine.

8. Adjust the seasoning, adding more salt and liquid smoke to taste. Serve warm, at room temperature, or chilled.

Creamy Coleslaw with Pineapple and Almonds

Serves 8-10 • *Prep. Time: 15 minutes* • *Chilling Time: 1 hour*

½ cup slivered almonds

2 cups shredded green cabbage

1 cup shredded carrots, *optional*

1 cup pineapple tidbits, fresh or canned

½ cup mayonnaise

½ cup sour cream

2 Tbsp. fresh lime juice

1 Tbsp. grated onion

2 tsp. sugar

salt to taste

1. Toast the almonds, spread out on a cookie sheet, in a 350° oven for 8-10 minutes until they are a warm brown. Set aside to cool.

2. In a large bowl, combine cabbage, carrots if you wish, pineapple, and almonds.

3. In a separate small bowl combine mayonnaise, sour cream, lime juice, onion, and sugar.

4. Taste for salt and sugar, adding more of each, as desired.

5. Toss with the salad ingredients and chill for at least one hour.

GUESTS WILL *be coming back for seconds and thirds of this deliciously fruity coleslaw!*

Magic Fudge Cake

Serves 12-16 • *Prep. Time: 20 minutes* • *Cooking/Baking Time: 40 minutes*

CAKE

2 cups all-purpose flour

2 cups sugar

1 tsp. cinnamon

2 tsp. baking soda

2 sticks (1 cup) butter, or margarine

2 Tbsp. unsweetened cocoa powder

1 cup water

2 eggs

½ cup buttermilk, or plain yogurt

1 tsp. vanilla

FROSTING

½ stick (¼ cup) butter

2 Tbsp. cocoa powder

¼ cup buttermilk, or whole milk

1 tsp. vanilla

2 cups powdered sugar

1. In a large bowl whisk together flour, sugar, cinnamon, and baking soda.

2. In a small saucepan, boil together butter, cocoa powder, and water.

3. In a separate small bowl, beat the eggs. Stir in the buttermilk and vanilla.

4. Stir the butter/cocoa/water mixture into the flour mixture with a wooden spoon.

5. Add the egg/buttermilk mixture and continue stirring to mix completely.

6. Pour into greased and floured 10"×15" rimmed baking sheet. Bake for 30 minutes at 350°.

7. Allow cake to cool. Make frosting, saving clean-up time by using saucepan from Step 2.

8. In a small saucepan, combine butter, cocoa powder, and milk. Bring to a boil.

9. Remove from the heat and stir in the vanilla and powdered sugar. Beat until smooth.

10. Spread over the cooled cake.

COOK'S NOTE
To substitute for buttermilk or plain yogurt, put 2 teaspoons lemon juice or cider vinegar into the measuring cup, add milk to the ½ cup mark. Let set for a few moments to curdle.

THIS CAKE *has been a family favorite ever since Ron's sister Ellie, introduced it to us years ago. We come back to it time after time because it's easy to put together and is practically no-fail. Serve the cake warm from the oven with ice cream or fudge sauce, or frost it to take to a potluck.*

A Not Quite Traditional Thanksgiving

Angel's Roast Turkey with Oranges

The Best Gravy

Roasted Sweet Potatoes with
Lime and Cilantro

Cornbread and
Sausage Dressing Casserole

Green Beans with Prosciutto

Fresh Cranberry Orange Relish

Pumpkin Streusel Pie

WHOSE IDEA WAS IT, anyway, to use the garden railroad as the centerpiece for the Thanksgiving dinner table? Ron and I each think it was our idea, but whoever first thought of it, the grandchildren loved it! It came about because there were more than 20 of us, and we were setting up the tables end to end, stretching from the doors of the study through the dining room and into the living room, with a 45-degree turn halfway along to accommodate the shape of the rooms. There was bound to be a problem passing the smaller items at such a long table.

The garden for Ron's railroad had not yet been established below our recently built house in Brown County, Indiana, so the tracks (including that lovely curve) came directly out of their boxes, shiny clean, and onto the center of the tables, stretching from end to end. Ron set up a control center under the table near the curve at the midway point. He practiced running the train up to one end of the table and down to the other, discovering that he needed a block at each end to prevent culinary disasters!

Very little additional decoration was needed on the tables. We used a few bright leaves scattered on the tablecloths along the tracks and the garden gauge train with its cars sitting proudly in the center, ready for service. Nothing more was required.

The open boxcars held the dinner rolls, the flatcars carried the butter, jam, salt, and pepper. The train chuffed along pleasantly after each call, bringing the needed items within easy reach of the guests. The children and the adults were equally entertained. We may not remember the menu for that Thanksgiving feast, but no one will ever forget the train!

The menu we've included here, while giving a nod to tradition without being quite traditional, is memorable, with or without a train for a centerpiece.

When Ron and I *returned to Puerto Rico last winter, Angel, who cares for our house there, had prepared us a welcome dinner. Angel, it turns out, is accomplished in the kitchen! One of his specialties is this incredibly flavorful Roast Turkey with Oranges, which he presented surrounded by roasted, garden-grown potatoes and carrots. The turkey was the best we'd ever tasted, and we eagerly requested the recipe. You don't have to wait for Thanksgiving, but if you do, this not-quite-traditional turkey will set a new standard for your celebration.*

Angel's Roast Turkey with Oranges

Serves 10-12 • Prep. Time: 30 minutes • Marinating Time: 12-36 hours
Baking Time: 5 hours • Standing Time: 30 minutes

ADOBO

7 large cloves garlic

¼ cup olive oil

3 Tbsp. salt

1 Tbsp. oregano

1 tsp. ground cumin

1 tsp. black pepper

1 tsp. vinegar

2 Tbsp. rum

6 oz. frozen orange juice
concentrate, undiluted

12-14 lb. turkey

½ cup fresh lemon juice

2 oranges, washed

1. Prepare the adobo. Crush the peeled garlic cloves with the side of a heavy knife and put in a medium bowl. Add the olive oil, salt, oregano, cumin, black pepper, vinegar, rum, and orange juice concentrate. Allow to stand for about an hour.

2. Prepare the turkey. Rinse the bird inside and out with cold water. Pat dry with paper towels. Sprinkle with lemon juice.

3. Loosen, but do not remove, the skin from the bird by running your fingers between the skin and the meat.

4. With a sharp knife, cut slits right down to the bone in the flesh of the thighs, legs, and breast, leaving the skin intact.

5. Now rub the adobo into the cuts and over all the flesh of the bird underneath the skin and inside the cavity. Stuff pieces of the garlic into the cuts.

6. Place on a rack in a roasting pan. Cover tightly with the lid and seal it in a plastic bag to keep the aromas inside. Refrigerate overnight or up to two days.

7. On the day of roasting, uncover the pan. Cut the two oranges in half and squeeze the juice all over the bird. Place the squeezed rinds inside the cavity.

8. Put the lid back on, or cover with foil. Roast in a preheated 350° oven for one hour. Lower the temperature to 325° and continue to roast about 4 hours, basting every 30-45 minutes with the pan juices or with more orange juice. Uncover the turkey for the last half hour to brown its surface. Turkey is done when meat thermometer inserted in deepest part of thigh registers 165°.

9. Remove the turkey to a cutting board. Cover loosely with foil. Let rest at least 30 minutes before slicing. Remove oranges from cavity and discard. Slice and serve.

The Best Gravy

Serves 12-16 • *Prep. Time: 10 minutes* • *Chilling Time: 4-5 hours* • *Cooking Time: 15 minutes*

turkey scraps such as neck,
wing tips, tail, and giblets
(do not include liver)

2 Tbsp. oil

1½ cups carrots, chopped

1½ cups onions, chopped

1 cup dry white vermouth,
or dry white wine

1-2 ribs celery

1 bay leaf

½ tsp. thyme

½ tsp. pepper

4 cups water plus
2 bouillon cubes,
or 4 cups canned
chicken broth

5 Tbsp. cornstarch

½ cup cold chicken broth,
or water

1. In a Dutch oven, brown the turkey scraps in oil until richly browned. Brown the liver separately to add to the finished gravy if you like giblet gravy, or save as a treat for the pets.

2. Add the carrots and onions to the Dutch oven and continue to brown.

3. When the vegetables are nicely browned, add the vermouth or white wine, and stir to deglaze the pan.

4. Add the celery, bay leaf, thyme, pepper, and the water and bouillon.

5. Simmer 1½ hours, partially covered.

6. Strain out the solids. Chill the broth until fat hardens on top, 4-5 hours. Skim excess fat.

7. Combine any pan juices with the defatted, refrigerated turkey stock to make 4 cups of liquid.

8. Heat turkey stock in medium saucepan until steaming.

9. Mix cornstarch with cold broth. Pour into hot turkey stock, stirring continuously.

10. Bring to a boil and boil for 1-2 minutes, stirring.

11. Check for salt and season to taste. Serve.

THIS GRAVY *is suitable with Angel's turkey, or with more traditional roast turkey recipes. It's also the best gravy recipe to use when roasting other types of poultry, such as chicken or quail.*

The day before you roast the turkey, take the neck, the giblets, cut off the wing tips to the second joint – why not take the tail, too? The more pieces the better.

Roasted Sweet Potatoes
with Lime and Cilantro

Serves 8-12 • *Prep. Time: 15 minutes* • *Baking Time: 25-30 minutes*

6 medium sweet potatoes, peeled and cut into 1" pieces

6 Tbsp. olive oil, *divided*

1 tsp. salt, *divided*

¼ tsp. cayenne

freshly ground black pepper, to taste

1 tsp. finely grated lime zest

2 Tbsp. fresh lime juice

⅔ cup chopped fresh cilantro

1. Toss the sweet potatoes with 4 Tbsp. oil and ½ tsp. salt in a shallow baking pan.

2. Arrange potatoes in one layer and roast at 425°, stirring halfway through roasting, until tender, about 25 minutes total. To make them crisper and browner, slip them under the broiler for a few minutes.

3. While the potatoes are roasting, prepare the dressing. In a small bowl, whisk together remaining 2 Tbsp. oil, remaining ½ tsp. salt, cayenne, pepper, lime zest, and lime juice. Set aside.

4. Remove the potatoes from the oven and scrape them into a serving bowl.

5. Pour the dressing over the potatoes. Stir gently to combine completely.

6. Sprinkle with cilantro before serving.

THESE SWEET POTATOES *are the perfect side dish for our not-quite-traditional Thanksgiving dinner, but we're pretty sure you'll be making them more than just once a year. They're little bites of caramelized smoothness, binding sweet, tart, and salty flavors together with fresh cilantro. Family members rave about this recipe.*

Cornbread and Sausage Dressing Casserole

Serves 12 • Prep. Time: 45 minutes • Cooking/Baking Time: 2 hours

THE CORNBREAD

3½ cups all-purpose flour

1½ cups cornmeal

¼ cup sugar

4 tsp. baking powder

1¼ tsp. salt

2 cups whole milk

½ cup vegetable oil

4 large eggs

1. Whisk flour, cornmeal, sugar, baking powder, and salt in a large bowl to blend.

2. Whisk milk, oil, and eggs in a separate medium bowl to blend.

3. Add the milk mixture to dry ingredients. Stir until evenly moistened.

4. Transfer batter to greased 9"×13" baking pan.

5. Bake cornbread at 400° until edges are golden brown and tester comes out clean, about 25 minutes. Cool completely in pan. Cover and store at room temperature up to 2 days.

WE CALL THIS *a casserole because we don't stuff the bird with it. To make it, you'll need a pan of cornbread, so bake this a day or two before the big meal. In fact, you could prepare the whole casserole ahead of time, up to Step 8 in the recipe.*

Cornbread and Sausage
Dressing Casserole (continued)

THE DRESSING CASSEROLE

2 lbs. spicy bulk sausage

1 cup (2 sticks) butter

3 cups chopped celery

3 cups chopped onions

3 cups peeled, chopped
Granny Smith apples

2 Tbsp. dried sage, or
4 Tbsp. chopped fresh sage

1 cup chopped fresh parsley

2 tsp. poultry seasoning

1½ tsp. salt

1 tsp. ground black pepper

16 cups crumbled
cornbread, not packed

4 large eggs, beaten

1 cup chicken broth

⅔ cup frozen apple juice
concentrate, thawed

1. Sauté sausage in heavy large skillet over medium-high heat, breaking up finely with back of fork, about 10 minutes. Sausage should not be pink in middle.

2. Using a slotted spoon, transfer sausage to a very large bowl.

3. Pour out any accumulated drippings in the skillet. Melt butter in the same skillet over medium high heat.

4. Add the celery, onions, apples, and sage. Sauté until very tender, about 12 minutes.

5. Add this to the sausage, along with the parsley, poultry seasoning, salt, and pepper. Stir to combine.

6. Add cornbread to sausage mixture. You can stop at this point and refrigerate, well-covered, until time to bake. Then continue with Step 7 before baking.

7. In a separate bowl, whisk the eggs, chicken broth, and apple juice concentrate.

8. Combine the egg mixture with the cornbread and sausage mixture.

9. Transfer to a large, deep, greased casserole or two medium casseroles. Cover with foil.

10. Bake the casserole, covered, alongside the turkey at 325° for 45-60 minutes.

11. Uncover and continue baking until top is golden, about 30 minutes more.

COOK'S NOTE
You can make your own poultry seasoning by combining equal amounts of dried thyme, sage, oregano, marjoram, and rosemary, then grinding to a powder in a spice grinder. You could also include proportionally smaller amounts of black pepper and nutmeg to your mix.

217

Green Beans with Prosciutto

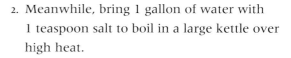

Serves 12 • Prep. Time: 15 minutes • Cooking Time: 20-25 minutes

COOK'S NOTE

You can substitute bacon, finely diced, in which case omit the olive oil.

2 Tbsp. olive oil

4 oz. thin-sliced prosciutto, chopped

2 small onions, finely chopped

2 cloves garlic, finely chopped

3 lbs. green beans, washed, stem ends trimmed

salt, to taste

1. In a large frying pan over medium-high heat, add the oil, prosciutto, onion, and garlic. Fry, stirring frequently, until onion is translucent and lightly browned, about 10 minutes.

2. Meanwhile, bring 1 gallon of water with 1 teaspoon salt to boil in a large kettle over high heat.

3. Add beans and cook, uncovered, until tender-crisp when pierced, 6-12 minutes, depending on variety.

4. Drain the beans, taste for salt, and place in a serving dish (or follow directions below for serving the next day).

5. Pour the prosciutto and onion mixture over the beans. Toss to coat evenly. Serve.

COOK'S NOTE

If preparing the day before serving, have a large bowl of ice-water ready while you cook the beans. Drain the beans when they are crisp-tender (as above) and immediately immerse in the ice water. Chill, airtight, until needed. Reheat in boiling water for 2-3 minutes. Drain beans, add salt to taste, and place in a serving dish. Pour over the onion mixture to serve. The onion mixture can also be made a day ahead and reheated just before combining with the beans to serve.

YOU CAN PREPARE *these beans the day before you serve them, so if it's a dinner party, get a head start. Since this recipe is for 12 servings, you'll want to cut it in half for a family meal.*

Fresh Cranberry Orange Relish

Serves 8-10 • *Prep. Time: 10 minutes*

16-oz. pkg. fresh or frozen cranberries

1 orange, zest and juice

1 cup sugar, or more, to taste, *divided*

1. In your food processor, process the cranberries with the zest, the juice, and half the sugar, until finely chopped.

2. Taste the relish. Add additional sugar to taste.

3. Cover and refrigerate until time to serve.

DON'T SKIP THIS *addition to your Thanksgiving feast. The fresh tang of the sauce is the perfect accompaniment to all the rich dishes. And don't forget all the health benefits of this versatile berry packed with antioxidants!*

This relish is actually better the second day, so make it ahead if you can. What could be easier?

Granddaughters love to make music at Sibyl's piano. Left to right: Evelyn, Mia, and Maddie.

FOR A NEW TWIST *on the traditional pumpkin pie, try this recipe with the walnut streusel topping. Serve it slightly warm with a dollop of whipped cream....delicious!*

Pumpkin Streusel Pie

Serves 6-8 • *Prep. Time: 20 minutes* • *Baking Time: 35-40 minutes* • *Cooling Time: 2 hours*

1 cup firmly packed brown sugar, *divided*

½ cup rolled oats

½ cup chopped walnuts

5 Tbsp. all-purpose flour, *divided*

half stick (¼ cup) butter

2 tsp. cinnamon, *divided*

1 tsp. nutmeg, *divided*

½ cup granulated sugar

¼ tsp. ground ginger

½ tsp. salt

15-oz. can pumpkin

12-oz. can evaporated milk

2 large eggs, beaten

10" pie shell for a single crust pie
(see page 15)

⚠ COOK'S NOTE

If you only have a 9" pan, you'll have too much custard to fit the crust. Bake the extra pumpkin custard in two custard cups.

1. Make the Walnut Streusel. Mix together ½ cup brown sugar, oats, walnuts, 4 Tbsp. flour, butter, ½ tsp. cinnamon, and ½ tsp. nutmeg. Mix until crumbly, using fingers or a pastry blender. Set aside.

2. Make the pumpkin custard. In a bowl, mix granulated sugar, ½ cup brown sugar, 1 Tbsp. flour, 1½ tsp. cinnamon, ½ tsp. nutmeg, ginger, and salt.

3. Add pumpkin, milk, and eggs. Whisk until well blended

4. Pour mixture into unbaked pastry shell.

5. Sprinkle walnut streusel evenly over filling.

6. Bake on the bottom rack of a 375° oven until center barely jiggles when pan is gently shaken, 35-40 minutes.

7. Set on rack until cool to touch, about 2 hours. Serve with whipped cream or vanilla ice cream.

CHAPTER 14

Brunch on the Deck

Mom's Granola

Broccoli and Feta Cheese Pie

Polenta

Polenta with Roasted Red Peppers

Creamy Corn Bake (see page 18)

Ellen's Favorite Spinach Quiche

Graham Streusel Coffee Cake

Ricotta Cheese and Paneer

Sweet Ricotta Fritters

Almond Twists with Browned Butter Icing

THE FIRST TIME we served brunch on the deck of our new house in the woods, the air was balmy and inviting, and the sun sparkled on the lake below us, creating patterns of leafy shade on our tables. The out-of-doors was the perfect place for young grandchildren with platefuls of food!

We still find that sunny mornings on the deck are the ideal setting for a brunch. The dishes included here are not a menu, but a collection of the recipes we turn to whenever we plan for a group, choosing two or three of the casseroles for the buffet, depending on the number of guests. A separate table is set up for the juices, tea, and coffee. These casseroles, many of which can be prepared in advance, would also serve well for a lunch or dinner main dish. Any of the breads could double as dessert, as well as being perfect for serving at an afternoon tea.

THIS HAS BECOME *a family favorite staple which some of us simply cannot live without. We think this granola is even better than the specialty granolas found at the market, and much more economical! It's delicious on its own in a bowl with milk, but it's absolutely amazing when stirred into plain yogurt and drizzled with honey and fresh fruit.*

I've often made this without the soybeans, pumpkin seeds, and flax seeds, which I couldn't get in Puerto Rico. I also substituted all-purpose flour when I couldn't get the whole wheat.

Give the recipe your own signature by using different nuts and adding dried fruit combinations to the finished granola. You might add cinnamon, coconut milk, or a touch of brown sugar...the variations are endless.

Mom's Granola

Prep. Time: 20 minutes • Baking Time: 60-80 minutes • Cooling Time: 1-2 hours

1 cup vegetable oil

1 cup honey, or ½ cup honey and ½ cup real maple syrup

¼ cup water

½ tsp. salt

1-2 tsp. vanilla

2½ cups rolled oats

2½ cups quick oats

1 cup whole wheat flour

2 cups shredded coconut

2 cups coarsely chopped nuts (walnuts or pecans are our favorites)

1 cup sunflower seeds

1 cup pumpkin seeds

1 cup dry-roasted soy nuts

½ cup sesame seeds

½ cup flax seeds, *optional*

1 cup wheat germ, *optional*

1. In a small bowl combine well the oil, honey, water, salt, and vanilla.

2. In a separate large bowl, combine all the dry ingredients – oatmeal through wheat germ.

3. Toss the dry ingredients with the oil/honey mixture until they are completely moistened. If it seems too dry, combine a little more oil and honey to add to the mix.

4. Spread in two large baking pans and bake at 325°.

5. Take your pans out of the oven every 15 to 20 minutes to stir, and alternate your pans from top to bottom in the oven. This can take an hour or more, since you want the granola to be a rich, deep brown. Hang around the kitchen, or set your timer so you don't forget to keep stirring it!

6. Return the pans to the oven, door ajar, and let them cool with the oven. Cool completely before storing the granola in jars or plastic containers.

THIS GREEK-INSPIRED CASSEROLE is a great vegetarian main dish, combining vegetables, eggs, and cheese. I discovered that it freezes well, too, when I served re-heated portions along with bread and crackers as part of a soup supper. The tasty little morsels were such a hit that I wished I'd saved back more!

Broccoli and Feta Cheese Pie

Serves 8-10 • *Prep. Time: 40 minutes* • *Cooking/Baking Time: 1 hour* • *Cooling Time: 10 minutes*

2 lbs. fresh broccoli, about 1 large head

half stick (¼ cup) butter

½ cup finely chopped onion

3 eggs

½ lb. feta cheese, crumbled

¼ cup chopped parsley

2 Tbsp. chopped fresh dill

½ tsp. salt

dash pepper

8 phyllo pastry sheets, thawed as package directs

1 stick (½ cup) butter, melted, for brushing the phyllo

1. Wash the broccoli and coarsely chop the stems, leaves, and flowerets.

2. Turn chopped broccoli into a large skillet. Add ½ cup boiling water. Cook, covered, over medium heat for 5 minutes. Drain well. Remove from the skillet and set aside.

3. Wipe out the pan. In it sauté the chopped onion in ¼ cup butter, stirring until it is golden, about 3 minutes.

4. Add chopped broccoli. Sauté 1 minute, stirring continually. Remove from heat.

5. In a large bowl, beat eggs slightly.

6. Add feta cheese, chopped parsley and dill, salt, pepper, and broccoli mixture. Mix well.

7. Line inside of a 9" springform pan with 6 phyllo pastry sheets, overlapping edges. Brush each sheet with melted butter before putting it in the pan. Let the excess pastry hang out over the edge of the pan.

8. Pour broccoli filling into the prepared pan. Fold overlapping edges of pastry sheets over top of filling.

9. With scissors, cut four 9" circles from remaining phyllo leaves. If needed, use a 9" cake pan as a guide.

10. Brush each circle with melted butter. Lay all 4 circles on top of the pie.

11. With scissors, cut through the 4 phyllo circles to make 8 or 10 pie sections in the top. Pour any remaining butter over it.

12. Place the springform pan on a jellyroll pan to catch drippings (otherwise you'll have a kitchen full of smoke).

13. Bake 40-45 minutes at 350°, or until crust is puffy and golden brown. Remove to rack and cool 10 minutes.

14. When ready to serve, remove the side of the pan. With sharp knife, follow the precut lines and slice down to bottom crust to make 8 or 10 wedges.

Polenta

Serves 8 • Prep. Time: 5 minutes • Cooking Time: 15-30 minutes • Chilling Time: 2-4 hours

4 cups cold water, *divided*

1 cup cornmeal

1 tsp. salt

1. Bring 3 cups water to a boil in a large, preferably non-stick, saucepan with a lid.

2. In the meantime, in a small bowl combine the cornmeal, salt, and remaining 1 cup of cold water.

3. As soon as the water in the saucepan boils, pour in the cornmeal/salt/water mixture all at once, and stir constantly until it thickens. Be prepared with the lid because the polenta will splatter when it comes to a boil. Cover immediately when it begins to bubble.

4. Turn heat to very low, and cook for 5 minutes. Stir frequently. The coarse cornmeal takes at least 20 minutes.

5. Line a small loaf pan with plastic wrap, extending over the sides so you can wrap the polenta. Pour the hot polenta into the prepared pan and cover with the plastic wrap. Chill for 2-4 hours.

Left to right: Niles and Simon, Ann's sons, on the paddleboard in Sibyl's pond.

Polenta with Roasted Red Peppers

Prep. Time: 25 minutes • Baking Time: 35 minutes

3 large red bell peppers,
or one large (15-oz.) jar
roasted red peppers

14.5-oz can chopped
tomatoes with garlic and
basil, undrained

fresh basil, minced, or 1-2
Tbsp. basil pesto, to taste
(see page 44)

salt, to taste

1½ cups shredded cheese,
your choice

16-oz. tube polenta,
or your own, as on
page 228, chilled

fresh basil leaves, left whole,
optional

1. Roast the peppers following the instructions on page 133. Cut them into strips and set aside.

2. Drain the tomatoes in a sieve over a bowl, reserving the liquid.

3. Heat a large skillet over medium low heat. Add tomatoes. Cook 1 minute to concentrate the tomato flavor.

4. Gradually add tomato liquid. Simmer 1 minute.

5. Add bell pepper strips. Simmer 5 minutes.

6. Add the minced basil and/or pesto. Add salt to taste.

7. Slice the chilled polenta into ½" thick slices.

8. Assemble the casserole. Spread ¼ cup of the sauce in the bottom of a shallow 9"×13" baking dish.

9. Arrange overlapping slices of polenta over the sauce. (You may have extra slices.) Spread remaining pepper sauce over the top. Sprinkle evenly with the shredded cheese.

10. Bake at 350° for 25 minutes. Garnish with fresh basil leaves to serve, if desired.

229

Ellen's Favorite Spinach Quiche

Serves 6 • Prep. Time: 25 minutes • Cooking/Baking Time: 1 hour • Cooling Time: 10 minutes

10" deep-dish pie crust
(see page 15)

3 cloves garlic, minced

1 small red onion, diced

2 Tbsp. olive oil

10 oz. fresh curly leaf or
baby spinach, chopped

2 cups sliced mushrooms

½ tsp. salt, or to taste

black pepper, to taste

6 oz. crumbled feta cheese

2 oz. shredded cheddar
cheese

4 eggs, beaten

1 cup whole milk

2 small tomatoes, sliced

1. In a large skillet over medium heat, sauté garlic and onion in olive oil until the onion is translucent.

2. Stir in the chopped spinach and the mushrooms. Cook until spinach is wilted. Remove from heat.

3. Season generously with salt and pepper. Cool slightly.

4. Add feta and cheddar cheeses.

5. In a medium bowl whisk eggs and milk together.

6. Combine thoroughly with spinach mixture.

7. Pour into pie crust. Spread evenly as needed.

8. Place tomatoes on top.

9. Bake 45-50 minutes at 375° or until center is set. Cool 10 minutes before serving.

THIS WONDERFUL COMBINATION *of spinach, cheeses, and mushrooms with a colorful tomato topping is a great addition to a brunch menu. It's also become a favorite supper entrée for Ellen's family.*

Graham Streusel Coffee Cake

Serves 12-16 • *Prep. Time: 25 minutes* • *Baking Time: 45-50 minutes* • *Cooling Time: 1-2 hours*

THE STREUSEL

2 cups graham cracker crumbs

1 cup chopped nuts

¾ cup packed brown sugar

1½ tsp. cinnamon

1½ sticks (¾ cup) butter, melted

THE CAKE

2 cups all-purpose flour

2 cups sugar

3 tsp. baking powder

½ tsp. salt

1 stick (½ cup) butter, melted

½ cup vegetable oil

2 cups plain yogurt

2 eggs, beaten

THE GLAZE

1 cup powdered sugar

1-2 Tbsp. water

¼ tsp. vanilla

1. Combine the graham cracker crumbs, nuts, brown sugar, cinnamon, and melted butter. Set aside.

2. Prepare the cake batter. In a large bowl, whisk together the flour, sugar, baking powder, and salt.

3. In a separate bowl whisk together the butter, vegetable oil, yogurt, and eggs.

4. Fold the wet mixture into the dry mixture, combining gently. Then stir vigorously with a wooden spoon until it is smooth and silky.

5. Pour half of batter into a greased and floured 9"×13" baking pan.

6. Sprinkle half the prepared streusel over the batter in the pan.

7. Spread the remaining batter evenly over the streusel layer.

8. Top with the remaining streusel.

9. Bake at 350° for 45-50 minutes, or until toothpick inserted in middle comes out clean. Cool.

10. Meanwhile, prepare the glaze. Combine the powdered sugar, 1 Tbsp. water, and vanilla in a small bowl. Add more water if needed to thin the glaze.

11. Drizzle glaze over finished, cooled cake.

> **COOK'S NOTE**
> *You could substitute a yellow cake mix for the yogurt cake in this recipe, (but it won't be as good!). Prepare according to package directions and follow the steps above.*

THE YOGURT CAKE *that is the basis of this coffee cake is a recipe you'll want to repeat again and again, with or without the streusel. Try serving it on its own with fresh berries and whipped cream. It is a delicious, moist cake with a bit of a tang and a snap to make – a big winner in our family.*

Ricotta Cheese and Paneer

Chilling Time: 3 hours • Prep. Time: 5 minutes • Cooking Time: 10-15 minutes

8 cups whole milk

1 cup cream or half-and-half

1 tsp. salt

3 Tbsp. lemon juice

EQUIPMENT

a colander

cheesecloth

large, heavy saucepan

medium bowl

slotted spoon or
mesh skimmer

1. Line a colander with 4 layers of cheesecloth. Place in sink.

2. Bring milk, cream, and salt to a simmer, just ready to break into a full boil, in a heavy, large saucepan over medium-high heat.

3. Stir in lemon juice. Lower heat. Let simmer until curds form, 1-2 minutes.

4. Using a finely slotted spoon or skimmer, scoop curds from pan and transfer to cheesecloth-lined colander. Let drain 1 minute – curds will still be a little wet. Let the curds drain only for the amount of time specified for the moistest, lightest consistency.

5. Transfer curds to medium bowl. Cover and chill until cold, about 3 hours. This will keep in the refrigerator for several days.

COOK'S NOTE

If you want to make paneer (Indian white cheese), drain the cheese longer. Gather up the cheesecloth around the cheese, tie it to the sink faucet, and let it drain 30 minutes. Shape into a round, flattened disc, still in the cheesecloth. Lay on a board tilted toward the sink to drain further with the twisted cloth edges to one side, out of the way, and with a weight on top for 30 more minutes. Use a flat plate with a can of food on top as a weight. Remove the cheesecloth and cut as desired. Store the paneer in an airtight container in the refrigerator 4-5 days, or freeze up to 4 months.

D**ID YOU KNOW** *that ricotta cheese is easy to make? If you've never tasted fresh ricotta, now is the time to give yourself a treat. It takes about 15 minutes and a half gallon of whole milk to make 1½ cups of ricotta. Drain it longer, apply weights, and you've produced paneer, the Indian cheese you need for Spinach and Paneer (see page 176 for recipe).*

Sweet Ricotta Fritters

Serves 6-8 • *Prep. Time: 15 minutes* • *Cooking Time: 10-15 minutes*

3 cups vegetable oil

3 eggs

¼ cup sugar

1 cup ricotta cheese
(see page 232)

½ tsp. vanilla

1¼ cups all-purpose flour

2 tsp. baking powder

⅛ tsp. salt

powdered sugar

1. Place the oil in a saucepan and heat to 375°, or close to that.

2. In a mixing bowl, beat the eggs. Add the sugar and beat until light.

3. Add the ricotta and vanilla. Mix well.

4. In a separate bowl, mix the flour, baking powder, and salt. Stir into the egg and cheese mixture.

5. Drop by scant teaspoonfuls into the hot oil. Keep them small so the centers get done. Just watch how they flip themselves over when they're ready!

6. When they've cooked a few minutes on the second side and are nicely browned, scoop them out with a slotted spoon. Drain briefly on paper towels, transfer to a serving plate, and sift powdered sugar over generously.

Almond Twists with Browned Butter Icing

Serves 8-10 • *Prep. Time: 35 minutes* • *Chilling Time: 2-24 hours*
Rising Time: 1 hour • *Baking Time: 20 minutes*

2¼ cups all-purpose flour

1 Tbsp. (1 package)
rapid-rise instant yeast

1 tsp. salt

1 stick (½ cup) cold butter,
cut into ½" cubes

1 large egg

¼ cup warm (110°)
evaporated milk

¼ cup warm (110°) water

2 Tbsp. sugar

3 Tbsp. butter, melted, *divided*

½ cup light brown sugar,
packed

⅔ cup sliced almonds, *divided*

1. Pulse the flour, yeast, and salt in a food processor until blended.

2. Add the cubed, cold butter and pulse until the flour is pale yellow and resembles coarse cornmeal. Turn mixture into a large bowl.

3. In a separate medium bowl, beat egg with milk, water, and sugar.

4. Using a rubber spatula, fold the milk mixture into the flour mixture. The dough will be sticky.

5. Divide the dough into two pieces. Wrap tightly in plastic wrap. Refrigerate until well chilled, at least 2 hours and up to 24 hours.

6. Make the filling. Toast almonds in a single layer on a cookie sheet in a 350° oven for 8-10 minutes until a rich, warm brown. Cool.

7. Mix brown sugar with ½ cup toasted almonds. Reserve rest of almonds for garnish. Set aside.

8. Working with one piece of dough at a time, roll the dough out on a floured board to a 14"×9" rectangle.

9. Brush the dough with half the melted butter. Sprinkle with half the almond filling mixture.

10. Starting at the long side, roll the dough into an even cylinder. Pinch the dough to seal. Transfer to a greased baking sheet, seam side down.

11. Using your kitchen shears, cut the cylinder of dough at 1" intervals, not cutting completely through. Leave about ¼" uncut at the bottom, so the slices are all still attached to each other.

12. Now fan out the slices, twisting each slice, first slice to the right, the next slice to the left, and so on, continuing to alternate slices the length of the cylinder.

13. Repeat with remaining dough.

14. Cover with plastic wrap coated with cooking spray. Let rise until the dough is almost doubled in size, about 1 hour.

15. Heat oven to 350°, with racks adjusted to middle upper and middle lower positions. Bake about 20 minutes, rotating and switching the baking sheets halfway through baking.

16. Cool until just warm. Make the Browned Butter Icing while the twists cool (recipe below). Drizzle icing over warm twists.

BROWNED BUTTER ICING

2 Tbsp. butter

1 cup powdered sugar

2 Tbsp. milk

1. Heat the butter in a small saucepan over medium heat, swirling the pan constantly, until the butter is golden brown, 3-5 minutes. Watch it closely. You want it richly browned, but not burned black!

2. Add the browned butter and milk to the powdered sugar. Blend until smooth with a spoon.

A LOVELY ALTERNATIVE *to the usual cinnamon rolls: no kneading, no cinnamon, and you won't miss it! When you have your first bite of this light, flaky roll, you'll love the way the browned butter flavor in the frosting combines with the toasted almonds of the filling. Be extravagant with the toasted almonds and sprinkle extra on top after you've iced the twists.*

Favorite Christmas Goodies

Coconut-Lime Bars

Honey Cayenne Pecans

Chocolate Truffles

Jane's Super Double Chocolate Cookies

EVERY FAMILY has their favorite treats to repeat every year at Christmas. The recipes in this section represent a few of the tried and true treats that make our Christmas goodie-tray year after year, and sometimes, when we can't hold out that long, in between times, too! The Christmas goodie-tray is a highly anticipated tradition.

A few new ones have made the list in the last year or two. To have a good variety we bake them days ahead of time and freeze them.

Coconut-Lime Bars

Serves 14-16 • Prep. Time: 20 minutes • Baking Time: 35-40 minutes • Cooling Time: 30 minutes

2 cups all-purpose flour

4 Tbsp. sugar

⅛ tsp. salt

1 stick (½ cup) + 2 Tbsp. cold butter

4 eggs, well beaten

2 cups brown sugar, firmly packed

1 cup chopped nuts

3 cups flaked coconut

2 Tbsp. lime juice

zest from 2 limes

1½ cups powdered sugar

1. In a food processor, combine flour, sugar, salt, and butter until well combined. Press firmly into the bottom of a 10"×15" baking pan.

2. Bake at 350° for 15 minutes. Remove from the oven and set aside.

3. In a medium bowl, beat eggs. Beat in the brown sugar.

4. Stir in the nuts and coconut.

5. Mix well and spread over the baked layer.

6. Bake an additional 20-25 minutes. Be sure that the bars are "set" in the middle.

7. Meanwhile, combine the lime juice and lime zest with the powdered sugar. Spread over the hot bars.

8. Let cool for 30 minutes before cutting into small bars or squares.

THE COMBINATION *of coconut with fresh lime calls out "tropical paradise."*

Honey Cayenne Pecans

Makes about 4 cups • Prep. Time: 10 minutes
Cooking/Baking Time: 20-25 minutes • Cooling Time: 1 hour

½ stick (¼ cup) unsalted butter

½ cup light brown sugar, packed

1 Tbsp. honey

1 Tbsp. water

scant ½ tsp. salt

¼ -½ tsp. cayenne pepper

½-1 tsp. chili powder

3½-4 cups pecans

1. Line a baking sheet with foil. Spray lightly with cooking spray.

2. Melt butter in a medium nonstick skillet over medium-low heat.

3. Add the sugar, honey, water, salt, cayenne, and chili powder, stirring until sugar dissolves. Start with the lesser amounts of cayenne and chili powder, increasing if you like more kick.

4. Increase heat to medium-high.

5. Add the pecans and stir constantly until caramel turns deep brown, bubbles vigorously, and coats nuts, about 5 minutes.

6. Pour nut mixture onto prepared sheet. Spread the nuts to separate.

7. Transfer to oven and bake at 325° for 12-15 minutes. Cool completely.

8. Store airtight at room temperature, or refrigerate for longer storage.

THESE ARE WONDERFUL *for salads or with ice cream, and irresistible for snacking! Or for a nice little gift, wrap some in a cellophane bag and tie it with a pretty ribbon, or place in a tissue-lined decorative tin. Who wouldn't be happy to receive a gift like that?*

Chocolate Truffles

Makes approximately 5 dozen • Prep. Time: 30 minutes
Cooking Time: 10 minutes • Chilling Time: 4-5 hours or overnight

12-oz. semisweet chocolate

⅔ cup butter, at room temperature

⅓ cup coffee liqueur

4 egg yolks

powdered cocoa, or ground almonds

1. Melt chocolate in double boiler with half the butter (⅓ cup).

2. Mix in the coffee liqueur, stirring well to blend completely.

3. Add egg yolks, one at a time, blending thoroughly after each one.

4. Return pan to the double boiler over simmering water for 3 minutes, stirring constantly.

5. Transfer to bowl of electric mixer. Whip in remaining ⅓ cup butter, 1 tablespoon at a time.

6. Beat until fluffy.

7. Cover with plastic wrap and chill 4 to 5 hours or overnight.

8. Roll into cherry-sized balls. Roll the balls in cocoa or nuts to coat.

9. Keep refrigerated, or freeze in a container with waxed paper between layers.

THIS LUXURIOUS *chocolate confection is best made with a high quality semi-sweet or dark chocolate. They make a beautiful holiday gift and are heavenly with a cup of hot coffee.*

239

Jane's Super Double Chocolate Cookies

Make 3-4 dozen • Prep. Time: 25 minutes • Baking Time: 7-8 minutes • Chilling Time: 30 minutes

1¾ cups Ghirardelli bittersweet
chocolate chips

6 Tbsp. butter, *divided*

¼ cup unsweetened cocoa powder

1¼ cups all-purpose flour

1 tsp. baking powder

scant ½ tsp. salt

¾ cup brown sugar

¼ cup granulated sugar

2 eggs

1 tsp. instant coffee granules

1 tsp. vanilla

½-1 cup chopped walnuts

½ cup Nestle's semisweet
chocolate chips

1. Melt the bittersweet chocolate chips with 2 Tbsp. butter in a double boiler.

2. Whisk together the cocoa powder, flour, baking powder and salt. Set aside.

3. In a mixer bowl, cream the remaining 4 Tbsp. butter with the sugars until fluffy.

4. Add the eggs, one at a time, beating well after each addition.

5. Stir in the coffee granules, vanilla, and the melted chocolate mixture, mixing well.

6. Stir in the dry ingredients, just until mixed, and then the walnuts and the ½ cup semisweet chocolate chips. Cover and refrigerate for 30 minutes.

7. Drop the dough by rounded tablespoons onto cookie sheets lined with parchment paper, allowing about 2" between each.

8. Bake at 350° for 7-8 minutes. Allow to cool on the baking sheets briefly before removing to racks.

THE KIND OF CHOCOLATE *you use does make a difference in these incredible cookies. For the best, fudge-brownie-like cookie, be sure to start with the Ghirardelli bittersweet chips. The semisweet chips are best for mixing into the dough. If you like dark chocolate, this is your cookie!*

Index

Mom's Granola, 225

B

C

Penne with Eggplant, Tomatoes, Fresh Mozzarella, and Herbs, 85

R

Refried Beans, 156

RHUBARB

Grandma's Rhubarb Cream Pie, 55

RICE

Brown and Wild Rice Pilaf with Toasted
Pecans, 52

Mexican Rice, 157

Steamed Basmati Rice, 172

Turkish Ottoman Rice Casserole, 28

White Rice a la Caribe, 163

Yellow Rice Pilaf, 112

Ricotta Cheese and Paneer, 232

Rippled Ice Cream Sherbet Pie, 181

Roasted Beet & Goat Cheese Salad with
Balsamic Dressing, 30

Roasted Eggplant and Garlic Salad
(Kyopoulo), 193

Roasted Herbed New Potatoes (Pecheni
Kartofi), 199

Roasted Red Pepper, Almond, and Cilantro
Pesto, 69

Roasted Sweet Potatoes with Lime and
Cilantro, 215

Roasted Yams (Kumara) and Garlic Cloves,
132

Round Loaf (Pitka), 197

Rustic Italian Bread, 12

S

Salad with Herbs and Roasted Pumpkin
Seeds, 135

SALADS

Blender Vinaigrette, 100

Caribbean Salad Ensalada Mixta, 168

Creamy Coleslaw with Pineapple and
Almonds, 208

Cucumber Salad, 106

Dijon, Bacon, and Potato Salad, 207

Evie's Fresh Spinach Salad, 39

Grilled Romaine Salad, 45

Mediterranean Salad Platter, 113

Mixed Greens with Grapes and Citrus
Vinaigrette, 73

Pear and Gorgonzola Salad with Orange
Dressing, 11

Roasted Beet & Goat Cheese Salad with
Balsamic Dressing, 30

Roasted Eggplant and Garlic Salad
(Kyopoulo), 193

Salad with Herbs and Roasted Pumpkin
Seeds, 135

Shrimp and Kiwi Salad, 101

Snow White Salad (Snejanka), 194

Spinach Salad with Mushrooms, Croutons,
and Warm Lemon Dressing, 93

Strawberry & Goat Cheese Salad with
Raspberry Dressing, 54

Tomato, Cucumber, and Cheese Salad
(Shopska Salata), 195

Variation on a Capri Salad, 125

Wilted Spinach Salad with Hot Bacon
Dressing, 19

SEAFOOD, SALMON

Bourbon-Glazed Salmon with Sesame
Seeds, 51

Potato, Kale, and Sausage Soup, 9